A Portrait of
Elizabeth I

in the words of the Queen and her contemporaries

edited by Roger Pringle

Barnes & Noble Books   Totowa, New Jersey

Illustration research and design by Ikon
25 St Pancras Way, London NW1

Filmset in 'Monophoto' Ehrhardt by
Servis Filmsetting Ltd, Manchester
Printed in Great Britain by
Biddles Ltd, Guildford, Surrey
for Ward Lock Educational
116 Baker Street, London W1M 2BB
A member of the Pentos Group
Made in Great Britain

First published in the USA 1980 by
  Barnes & Noble Books
  81 Adams Drive
  Totowa, New Jersey 07512
  ISBN 0-389-20088-3

Title page:
Queen Elizabeth I
in her coronation robes,
painted *c.* 1559

Contents

Introduction

The aim of this book is to present a portrait of Queen
Elizabeth I, viewed against some of the main events of her
reign, and to create the picture mainly out of the words of the
Queen herself and her contemporaries.

The selection of documents in each section is based on an
anthology recital which was devised for presentation in the
Royal Shakespeare Theatre at the time of the Silver Jubilee of
Queen Elizabeth II in 1977, with the distinguished actress
Janet Suzman 'playing' the Queen's illustrious ancestor. The
present choice, however, is a much expanded version of the
theatre programme and, with introductions to each section, it
is designed primarily to provide an attractive introduction to
the first Elizabeth's reign for the pleasure of students and
general readers of history. Nevertheless, I hope the book will
serve in some instances the aim of the original selection and
be used for recitation or dramatic purposes.

I believe more school students would enjoy the study of
history if histrionic elements entered occasionally into its
teaching. With this in mind, I hope the book will sometimes
be used for exercises in which students are cast in various
roles and speak aloud or perform the extracts, either after
they have read the introductions or in conjunction with them.

Whether the book is studied for exams, read in an armchair
or used for spoken performances, I trust its Elizabethan
extracts will not wear the cold face of disembodied statements
but rather will come alive with the knowledge of the person,
place or time associated with them. May they be read as
though their writers had just finished giving shape to their
ideas and passions and the ink from their quills was still wet
upon the page. The introductions to the sections are intended

to help in achieving this effect and to provide a context in which to interpret and judge the writings.

The documents themselves are of many different kinds: accounts by contemporary historians; pronouncements by government officials; comments by politicians and ambassadors who witnessed at first hand the crowded events in the political arena; entries in the travel journals of foreign visitors whose curiosity often led them to note details of English life which otherwise would have gone unrecorded; the eloquence of poets and playwrights; the private musings of courtiers who sought the Queen's favour, and sometimes her love; and the letters, speeches and poems of the Queen herself which convey her views and emotions on many public and personal matters.

One can strive to imagine the varied situations in which these documents were written: to see the chroniclers of the reign, Camden, Holinshed and Stow, bent over their study writing-tables and working into the night, with the candles flickering over their books and manuscripts; to hear the slap of the sea on Drake's ship and the distant boom of cannon fire as he despatches a confident letter reporting his success in the Armada battle; to stand with Robert Wyngfield in the hall of Fotheringhay castle on that February morning of 1587 and watch the executioner's axe sever the head of Mary, Queen of Scots; to find Peter Wentworth on his feet in the House of Commons delivering his fearless words on free speech which shock most of his fellow members; to listen to the Cotswold shepherd, dressed in his smock, who gives a speech of welcome (doubtless well rehearsed) as the Queen enters Sudeley Castle; and to eavesdrop on Elizabeth herself: to watch her long hand moving across acres of parchment as she endlessly drafts and redrafts speeches to Parliament; or as she composes those tortuous letters which skilfully evade the demands of politicians and suitors alike; or as she writes her icily direct admonitions to courtiers and officials who have disobeyed her commands; above all, to experience the magical effect of her oratory on an audience, as she speaks to her troops at Tilbury or addresses her Members of Parliament.

Although the documents bring us face to face with some of the memorable people and events of Elizabethan England, the main focus is on the remarkable woman who presided over them all and the selection has been made to reveal various aspects of Queen Elizabeth's complex personality and to show the impact she made on some of the vital issues of her age. And what an age it was! The forty-four years of Elizabeth's reign have long stood out as one of the most significant chapters in the whole history of Britain. Today, however, we are probably more aware than previous generations of how her 'Golden Age' was not without its shadows. Historians have rightly reminded us that some of the Queen's policies failed to achieve their desired effects, while others only succeeded at considerable human cost. We are aware, too, of the Queen's own shortcomings and we are likely to view with some scepticism the monarchical myth-making in which she and certain of her subjects indulged. In particular, the glorification of her as a timeless deity and a heavenly goddess may strike us as being merely the bizarre trappings of a benevolent despotism. It is also not difficult to see something tragic as well as glorious about Elizabeth's life. Sir Walter Ralegh said memorably of her that she was a lady surprised by time, and the anthology of pieces collected in this book, following the full curve of Elizabeth's reign, gives weight to the credibility gap which opened in her last years between the concept of the 'Divine Eliza' and the increasingly aged, lonely and irritable figure who occupied the throne.

Yet, after proper due has been given to the debit side in history's account book, the Elizabethan age remains outstanding for its notable achievements in many fields of human activity. The establishment of the Church of England, Shakespeare's plays, and the beginnings of English colonization in America are but three of the profitable returns of the reign which have proved to be profoundly significant legacies. The fact that the Queen was involved in the creation of all three is a measure of the extraordinary influence she wielded on her nation's life: she played a leading part in the Church settlement; she founded the first royal company of professional actors and patronised other leading theatre companies, including the Lord Chamberlain's Men for whom Shakespeare acted and wrote; and she gave moral and financial support to colonizing ventures such as Sir Walter

Ralegh's expeditions to America in the 1580s which founded the first English colony in the territory named Virginia in honour of the Queen. The age itself in which these memorable achievements were accomplished would appropriately assume the name of 'Elizabethan' after the presiding genius of the times.

This modest book is glad to take its place amongst the large number of writings which have been inspired by Queen Elizabeth's compelling personality and by the vital and exuberant history of her reign. I should like to thank Carole Mason for typing it with her usual efficiency and patience, and my wife for reading the draft and making a number of helpful suggestions.

A note on the text The spelling and punctuation of the contemporary extracts have sometimes been modernized in the interests of clarity. A row of dots indicates an omission. The extracts have been given numbers in sequence and these are also referred to by the number in the margin in the introductions to each section.

R.P.

Signature of Queen Elizabeth I

The new Queen

Elizabeth was twenty-five years old when she rode into London in November 1558 to assume the English throne after the death of Queen Mary I. The new queen inherited a kingdom which was bitterly divided by religion, had recently been humiliated in war, and faced major economic and social problems. Contemporaries, however, looked to Elizabeth with a sense of relief and hope after the dismal failures of the previous reign.

1   Elizabeth's character had been shaped by her traumatic upbringing. As the daughter of King Henry VIII, she inherited much of her father's astuteness and autocratic manner. She had learned, too, that it was a highly dangerous business to be a member of a royal family in the turbulent world of sixteenth-century politics. She was still a baby when her mother, Anne Boleyn, was executed, and before she had reached twenty, the heads of her stepmother, her uncle and her cousin had rolled from the block. During the reign of her sister Mary, her life was beset with dangers. When Mary came to the throne in 1553 the country returned to Catholicism after the Protestant reign of the young Edward VI. Suspected of plotting against her sister and aiding her Protestant opponents, Elizabeth was imprisoned in the Tower of London. She was fully aware of the likelihood of her execution or murder but she survived the ordeal and was later released and placed under house arrest. Memories of those days when self-preservation was her paramount concern must have crossed Elizabeth's mind during her triumphal entry into London in 1558, especially when she visited the Tower itself where she prayed to God for sparing her life. It was not empty rhetoric

2   that she spoke.

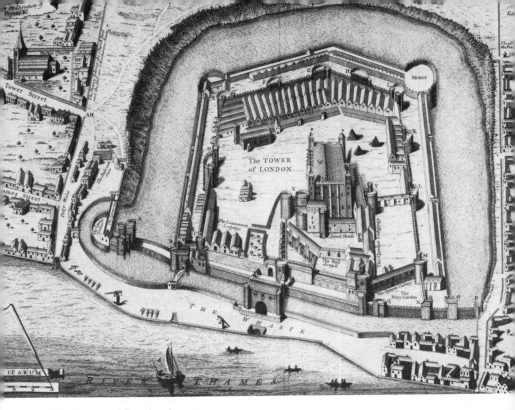

The Tower of London in 1597

The Queen's coronation in January 1559 was accompanied by great pageantry and cost over £16,000 to stage. The impressive ceremonies were designed to secure her succession to the throne and to win the allegiance of her subjects; but it was, above all, Elizabeth's charismatic personality which assured her of popular support in the first months of her reign. Contemporary observers witnessed the delighted reaction of people from all ranks of society to her winning ways.

Elizabeth came to the throne having acquired much political wisdom from her early years, especially from her experience of over-ambitious politicians during the reign of her brother, Edward VI, and from her knowledge of religion's disruptive force during Mary I's reign. She had also studied under several highly talented tutors who had developed her exceptional intelligence and gifts for learning. The most influential of her teachers was Roger Ascham who became one of the best-known educationalists of his time. The Queen's

brilliance of mind and powers of eloquence, often reflected in
her letters and speeches, owed much to the training she
received from Roger Ascham, who regarded her as his
4   brightest student and a model to inspire all young people.
    The euphoria which greeted the new queen on her accession
did not remove doubts and fears about the future felt by
some of her subjects. The Clerk of the Council jotted down a
short list of some of the serious problems facing the country,
and although his view may have been unduly pessimistic it
5   reflected the deep concern of many government officials.
    Some believed that the new monarch's sex would jeopardize
the chances of a successful reign. They did not regard the
harsh business of government as being a sympathetic task for
female rulers and supported their opinion by pointing to the
ill-fated reign of the late Queen Mary. John Knox, an
extremist Protestant, was an aggressive spokesman for this
view and even challenged the legitimacy of feminine rule,
couching his argument in excessively male-chauvinistic
6   language.

Traitors' Gate, Tower of London. Elizabeth was taken through here in 1554,
protesting her innocence

1 The Queen enters London 1558

Raphael Holinshed, one of the great historians of the new reign, recalled the optimistic mood of the times when Elizabeth rode into London to claim the throne.

After all the stormy, tempestuous, and blustering windy weather of Queen Mary was overblown, the darksome clouds of discomfort dispersed, the palpable fogs and mists of most intolerable misery consumed, and the dashing showers of persecution overpast, it pleased God to send England a calm and quiet season, a clear and lovely sunshine . . . and a world of blessings by good Queen Elizabeth, into whose gracious reign we are now to make an happy entrance as followeth . . .

At her entering the city, she was of the people received marvellous entirely, as appeared by the assemblies, prayers, wishes, welcomings, cries, tender words and all other signs, which argued a wonderful earnest love of most obedient subjects towards their sovereign. And on the other side, her grace, by holding up her hands and merry countenance to such as stood far off, and most tender and gentle language to those that stood nigh unto her grace, did declare herself no less thankfully to receive her people's good will, than they lovingly offered it to her. So that if a man would say well, he could not better term the City of London that time than a stage whereon was showed the wonderful spectacle of a noble hearted princess towards her most loving people, and the people's exceeding comfort in beholding so worthy a sovereign. . . .

2 The Queen's prayer at the Tower

. . . It is to be noted in her grace that for so much as God hath so wonderfully placed her in the seat of government of this realm, she in all her doing doth show herself most mindful of His goodness and mercy shewed unto her. And one notable sign thereof her grace gave at the very time of her passage through London, for in the Tower, before she entered her chariot,* she lifted up her eyes to Heaven and said as followeth:

'O Lord Almighty and everlasting God, I give Thee most hearty thanks that Thou hast been so merciful unto me as to spare me to behold this joyful day. And I acknowledge that Thou hast dealt as wonderfully and as mercifully with me as Thou didst with Thy true and faithful servant Daniel Thy prophet, whom Thou deliveredst out of the

* carriage

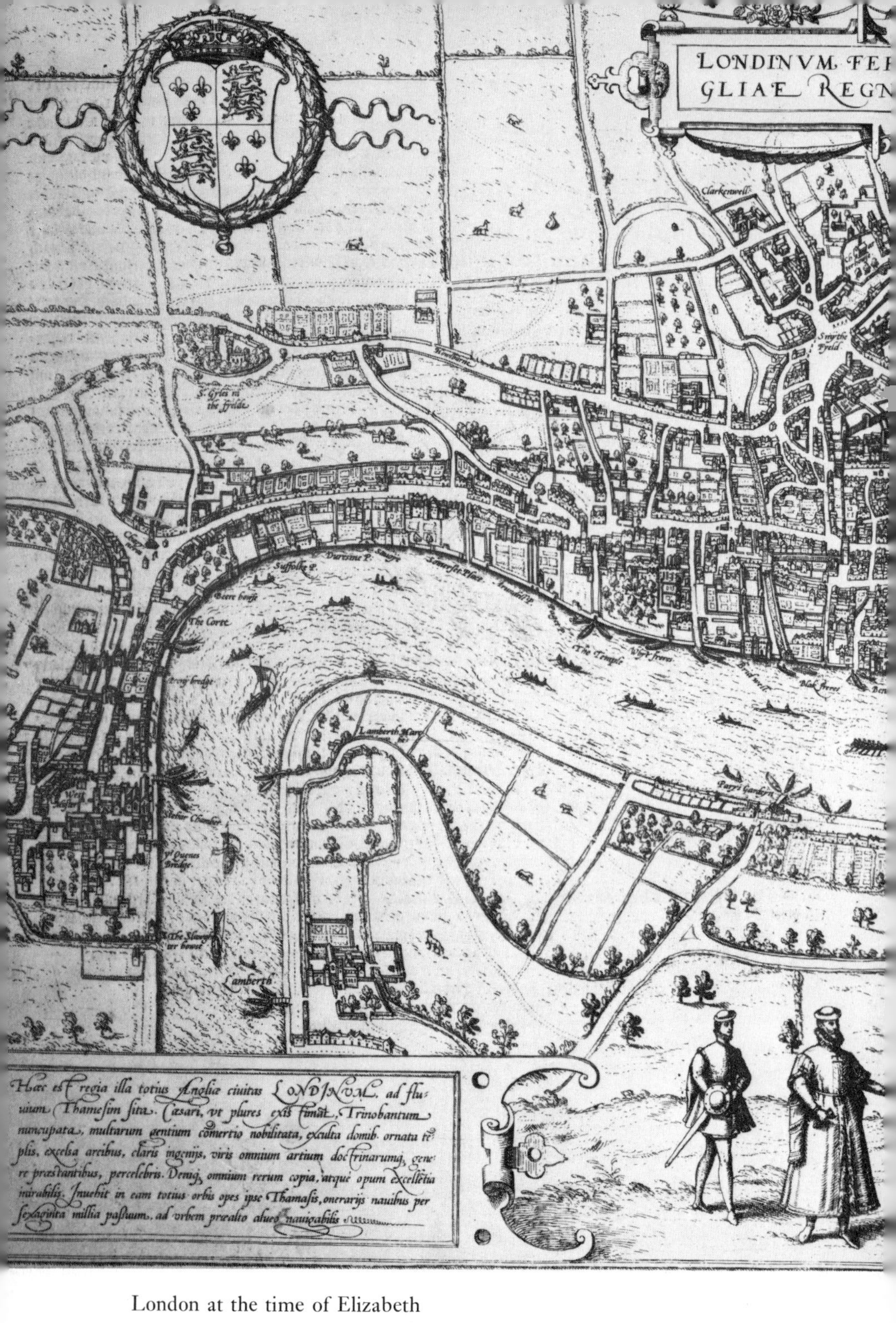

London at the time of Elizabeth

SIMI AN
TROPOLIS

The Spitel fields

The Towre

Cum Priuilegio.

STILLIARDS) Hansa, Gothica dictio, conuentum, vel congregationem sonans, multarum ciuitatum est confoederata Societas, tum, ob præstita Regibus, ac Ducib. beneficia: tum, ob securam terra, mariq́ue, mercaturæ tractationem, tum deniq́ue, ad tranquillam Rerumpub. pacem, & ad modestam adolescentium institutionem conseruandam, instituta: plurimoŕ Regum, ac Principum, maximè Angliæ, Galliæ, Daniæ, Magnæ Moscouiæ, nec non Flandriæ, ac Brabantiæ Ducum priuilegiis, ac immunitatib. exornata fuit. Habet ea quatuor Emporia, (untores quidam vocant, in quibus ciuitatum negotiatores resident, suasq́ue mercatus exercent. Hor̄. alterum hic Londini, domestica oeconomia nitet, habens domum Gildehallæ Teutonicā quā vulgò Stihard, nuncupā̄

den from the cruelty of the greedy and raging lions; even so was I
overwhelmed, and only by Thee delivered. To Thee, therefore, only be
thanks, honor, and praise, for ever.'

3 A portrait of the new Queen

**The first months of the reign were notable for the Queen's
success in captivating her people. Sir John Hayward described
the wonderful effectiveness of Elizabeth's 'performance' at the
time of her coronation and her personal appearance.**

Now, if ever any person had either the gift or the style to win the hearts of
people, it was this Queen; and if ever she did express the same, it was at
that present, in coupling mildness with majesty as she did, and in stately
stooping to the meanest sort. All her faculties were in motion, and every
motion seemed a well-guided action; her eye was set upon one, her ear
listened to another, her judgement ran upon a third, to a fourth she
addressed her speech; her spirit seemed to be everywhere, and yet so
entire in herself, as it seemed to be nowhere else. Some she pitied, some
she commended, some she thanked, at others she pleasantly and wittily
jested, contemning no person, neglecting no office; and distributing her
smiles, looks, and graces . . . that thereupon the people again redoubled
the testimonies of their joys . . .

   She was a Lady upon whom nature had bestowed, and well placed,
many of her fairest favours; of stature mean, slender, straight, and
amiably composed; of such state in her carriage, as every motion of her
seemed to bear majesty: her hair was inclined to pale yellow, her forehead
large and fair, a seeming seat for princely grace; her eyes lively and sweet,
but short-sighted; her nose somewhat rising in the middest; the whole
compass of her countenance somewhat long, but yet of admirable
beauty, not so much in that which is termed the flower of youth, as in a
most delightful composition of majesty and modesty in equal mixture.

4 The Queen's education

Elizabeth's tutor Roger Ascham praised her gifts of learning.

. . . The constitution of her mind is exempt from female weakness, and
she is endued with a masculine power of application. No apprehension
can be quicker than hers, no memory more retentive. French and Italian
she speaks like English; Latin, with fluency, propriety and judgment; she

also spoke Greek with me . . . The beginning of the day was always devoted by her to the New Testament in Greek, after which she read select orations of Isocrates and the tragedies of Sophocles, which I judged best adapted to supply her tongue with the purest diction, her mind with the most excellent precepts, and her exalted station with a defence against the utmost power of fortune . . .

It is your shame (I speak to you all, you young gentlemen of England), that one maid should go beyond you all, in excellency of learning and knowledge of divers tongues. Point forth six of the best given gentlemen of this court, and all they together shew not so much good will, spend not so much time, bestow not so many hours, daily, orderly and constantly, for the increase of learning and knowledge, as doth the Queen's Majesty herself. Yea I believe that, beside her perfect readiness in Latin, Italian, French and Spanish, she readeth here now at Windsor more Greek every day than some prebendary of this church doth read Latin in a whole week. And that which is most praiseworthy of all, within the walls of her privy chamber she hath obtained that excellence of learning, to understand, speak and write, both wittily with head and fair with hand, as

A book used by Roger Ascham to teach Latin to the young Elizabeth. Writing by Ascham is at the top of the page

scarce one or two rare wits in both the universities have in many years reached unto.

5 A pessimistic view of the kingdom's prospects

Armigail Waad, Clerk of the Council, wrote a gloomy summary of the problems at the start of Elizabeth's reign

The queen poor, the realm exhausted, the nobility poor and decayed. Want of good captains and soldiers. The people out of order. Justice not executed. All things dear. Excess in meat, drink and apparel. Divisions among ourselves. Wars with France and Scotland. The French king bestriding the realm, having one foot in Calais and the other in Scotland. Steadfast enmity but no steadfast friendship abroad.

6 The case against feminine rule

John Knox roused a clarion note of defiance to the new regime by arguing in his book *The First Blast of the Trumpet against the Monstrous Regiment of Women* that it was against natural and divine law for a woman to reign.

To promote a woman to bear rule, superiority, dominion, or empire above any realm, nation, or city, is repugnant to nature, contumely to God, a thing most contrarious to his revealed will and approved ordinance; and finally, it is the subversion of good order, or all equity and justice. . . . .

And first, where that I affirm the empire of a woman to be a thing repugnant to nature, I mean not only that God by the order of his creation hath spoiled woman of authority and dominion, but also that man hath seen, proved and pronounced just causes why that it should be. Man, I say, in many other cases blind, doth in this behalf see very clearly. For the causes be so manifest, that they cannot be hid. For who can deny but it be repugneth to nature that the blind shall be appointed to lead and conduct such as do see? That the weak, the sick, and impotent persons shall nourish and keep the whole and strong, and finally, that the foolish, mad and phrenetic shall govern the discreet and give counsel to such as be sober of mind? And such be all women, compared unto man in bearing of authority. For their sight in civil regiment is but blindness, their strength weakness, their counsel foolishness, and judgement frenzy, if it be rightly considered.

Government, monarchy and the court

The Elizabethans regarded society as part of a harmonious universe created by God in which all things were ordered according to degrees of superiority. The whole of creation – heaven, human societies and the animal kingdom – was structured in terms of degrees or ranks, and depended on the proper observance of place and precedence to avoid breaking down into anarchy. God was at the apex of the divine order and below were various ranks of angels, men and animals. Monarchs were believed to be God's representatives on earth and stood at the head of society. Below them were various classes, which owed obedience to their monarch and each man, in theory, took his rightful place in the hierarchical framework.

Like all Renaissance monarchs, Elizabeth derived much personal and political strength from the affirmation of these beliefs in the divine nature of monarchy and government. Coming to the throne as a young woman, she faced problems that threatened to drive the country towards chaos, and throughout her long reign there were few times when political intrigues and plots, or the threat of invasion from abroad, were not a danger. In such circumstances, governments grasped every opportunity to expound the hierarchical nature of society, and among the propaganda vehicles at their disposal was the use of homilies, or officially prepared sermons, which were required to be read aloud in every church in the land. The *Homily on Obedience*, setting forth the divine right of monarchs and the duties of subjects, was a forceful piece of political propaganda rather than a religious tract.

7   One of the most famous expositions of the hierarchical

nature of society is a speech by Ulysses, the Greek general, in
Shakespeare's play *Troilus and Cressida*. Ulysses argues that
the reason for the chaos in the Greek army and the lack of
success with their war against Troy is failure to observe order
and degree. The speech can be regarded as an indirect
indication that although the theory of an ordered society in
which each man had an appointed place was the conventional
wisdom of Shakespeare's own England, in practice society
was relatively fluid and there was considerable movement
between social classes. Indeed, the sensitivity of the
Elizabethans to status is reflected in the determination of
many of them to improve their position on the social ladder.
Yeomen scrambled to become gentlemen, gentlemen sought
knighthoods and knights and squires looked for entry into the
higher echelons of the aristocracy.

8

Elizabeth held an exalted opinion of her monarchical role,
believing that as God's representative on earth she wielded an
exclusive authority in affairs of state. She jealously protected
her right to make policy and to control the direction of
government, regarding the primary role of her chief ministers
and Parliament itself as being to give advice and to carry out
policies once she had devised and approved them. Fortunately
her autocratic view of government was accompanied by a flair
for making wise appointments of ministers. At the start of her
reign she chose Sir William Cecil, a thirty-eight-year-old
career politician, as her Principal Secretary. Cecil proved to
be not only an immensely hard-working bureaucrat but also a
man of political vision, with a capacity to grasp the complex
issues of government. He formed a remarkable working
partnership with Elizabeth which lasted for over thirty years
and it is impossible to decide which of the two contributed
more to the formulation of policy. He had the highest regard
for his sovereign and once wrote that she was 'the wisest
woman that ever was, for she understood the interests and
dispositions of all the princes in her time, and was so perfect
in the knowledge of her own realm, that no councillor she had
could tell her anything she did not know before'. Like most of
the Queen's councillors and subjects he shared Elizabeth's
lofty view of kingship and towards the end of his life he gave
advice on the obedience owed to a monarch to his son Robert

William Cecil later Lord Burghley, painted *c*.1585

Cecil who continued the family's political traditions and
9 served Elizabeth I and James I in high office.

The mainspring of Elizabeth's government was the Privy
Council which consisted of about a dozen of the most
prominent politicians. Apart from advising the Queen, this
was the chief administrative body in the realm and concerned
itself with a vast range of domestic, foreign and judicial
matters. Within the Council, Cecil (or Lord Burghley as he
became in 1571) found his position challenged by more
flamboyant rivals such as the Earls of Leicester and Essex.
Elizabeth shrewdly played off the personal rivalries and
differences which existed between her Councillors to maintain

Robert Dudley,
Earl of Leicester, 1576

her own independence of action, leading one contemporary,
Sir Robert Naunton, to write that the principal note of her
reign was that 'she ruled much by faction and parties which
herself both made, upheld, and weakened, as her own great
judgement advised'. It was much to her credit, however, that
she never allowed her personal affection for favourites like
Leicester and Essex to jeopardize Burghley's position as
principal adviser, and was quick to counteract any over-
ambitious political tendencies in them. In 1586 the Earl of
Leicester, after being sent to the Netherlands in charge of an
expedition against Spain, overstepped his authority by
appointing himself absolute governor of the Low Countries
without the consent of Elizabeth. The Queen immediately saw
the move as a potential threat to herself and sent him an
10   angry rebuke and a solemn warning.

Elizabeth made many wise appointments apart from
Burghley's. Sir Nicholas Bacon served her with distinction for
nearly twenty years as Lord Keeper of the Great Seal and Sir
Francis Walsingham was an outstanding Secretary of State
for seventeen years. Although the Privy Council was often
torn by divisions and rivalries between the leading ministers,
its collective wisdom and experience was exceptional. When
the Spanish ambassador seriously underestimated the
Council's quality and strength and wrote to Philip II in
derisive terms about some of its leading members, he was
doing a foolish disservice to his royal master, whose policy
11   towards England was much influenced by such reports.

Although there did not exist any modern democratic system

of elections, Parliament was considered to represent the whole
nation, and the Queen in Parliament was regarded as the
highest authority in the land. Laws were passed by the
Houses of Commons and Lords and their approval had to be
sought before new taxes could be levied. The centre of political
power, however, remained with the Queen and her Privy
Council and Parliament's role was in practice a restricted one.
It met on average only three weeks a year during Elizabeth I's
reign, and important areas of the national interest (such as
foreign policy, religious doctrine or practice and the
succession to the throne) lay, at least in the Queen's view,
outside its province. But during her reign, Parliament,
especially the House of Commons, became increasingly
unwilling to accept the Queen's limited view of its functions
and sought to play a more dynamic part in government by
initiating discussion of major issues and by shaping policy.
The Queen's attempt to restrict the freedom of the Commons
to debate matters of state was resisted by several strong-
minded and fearless Puritan members. One of them, Peter
Wentworth, rose to his feet in the 1576 Parliament, spoke
passionately in defence of free speech and went on to
denounce certain methods used by the Queen and her Council
to ensure members of the Commons observed the official
government line and refrained from debating sensitive issues
that were considered the Crown's prerogative. He singled out
for attack the practice of spreading rumours about the
Queen's anger whenever the members were veering from her
viewpoint or straying into prohibited areas of discussion, and
the device of sending messages to the Commons forbidding
debate on certain matters. Wentworth's bold challenge to the
autocratic nature of Elizabethan government resulted in his
being sent to the Tower.

Peter Wentworth's speeches highlighted a conflict between
the liberty of the individual and the authority of the state,
and reflected a small but growing opposition to the Crown's
stranglehold on government. Although only a handful of
members supported Wentworth's radical opinions, his was the
voice of the future and his speeches foreshadowed the conflict
between Parliament and the Crown which erupted after
Elizabeth's death and eventually led to civil war. While the

Queen reigned, however, the constitutional challenge of the Commons was checked, and her Lord Keeper's address to Parliament in 1593 reaffirmed her views on the limited rights of members to debate and legislate on matters regarded as

13 the Crown's prerogative.

The Queen's Court was the centre of the country's political and cultural life where business and pleasure were mixed in equal degrees. Men seeking office or advancement in public life went there, for the Crown was the ultimate source of political power and promotion. Writers, musicians and painters were attracted to it for the Court was a centre of arts and learning. High society gathered there to sport itself as the Court was still the focal point of the nation's social life. All activities revolved around and were linked to the Queen herself, the jewelled hub of a restless and glittering world. Magnificent pomp and ceremony accompanied the Court's routines, designed to foster a cult of monarchy and to elicit adulation for the Queen's figure. Apart from satisfying her natural vanity and taste for spectacle, the Court pageantry had much propaganda value in helping to impress its

14 authority on the kingdom.

The Queen turned her femininity to good effect in her desire to create a mystique of monarchy and to endow her high office with awe-inspiring and resplendent externals. On public occasions she dressed in gorgeous clothes and wore an array of dazzling jewellery. Precious stones sometimes dropped from her as she went on her walk-abouts and by the

15 end of her life she had over a thousand garments and dresses

16 in her Wardrobe.

The poets of Elizabeth's time wrote sheaves of verse in her praise, and often drew favourable comparisons between the Queen and famous examples of feminine beauty and virtue in classical literature or in the chivalric tales of the Middle Ages. Edmund Spenser's epic poem *The Faerie Queene*, an allegory based on the adventures of several knights, owed its central inspiration to Elizabeth herself who figures under various names in the poem. Its description of the enthroned queen in Book V is not essentially different from accounts written by visitors who travelled to Greenwich Palace or Hampton Court

17 and were dazzled by the majestic presence of Elizabeth.

7 The divine order of society

The *Homily on Obedience*, declaimed in the churches of
Elizabethan England, asserted the divine foundations of
monarchical government and the hierarchical nature of
society.

Almighty God hath created and appointed all things in heaven, earth, and
waters, in a most excellent and perfect order. In heaven He hath
appointed distinct and several orders and states of Archangels and Angels.
In earth He hath assigned and appointed Kings, Princes, with other
Governors under them, in all good and necessary order . . . Every
degree of people in their vocation, calling and office hath appointed to
them their duty and order: some are in high degree, some in low, some
Kings and Princes, some inferiors and subjects, priests and laymen,
masters and servants, fathers and children, husbands and wives, rich and
poor: and everyone hath need of other: so that in all things is to be lauded
and praised the goodly order of God; without the which no house, no city,
no commonwealth, can continue and endure, or last. For, where there is
no right order, there reigneth all abuse, carnal liberty, enormity, sin, and
Babylonical confusion. Take away Kings, Princes, rulers, magistrates,
judges and such estates of God's order; no man shall ride or go by the
highway unrobbed; no man shall sleep in his own house or bed unkilled;
no man shall keep his wife, children and possessions in quietness: all
things shall be common: and there must needs follow all mischief and
utter destruction both of souls, bodies, goods, and commonwealths.

8 Order and degree in society

Ulysses's speech from *Triolus and Cressida*, Act 1, scene 3, by
William Shakespeare.

The heavens themselves, the planets, and this centre,
Observe degree, priority, and place,
Insisture,* course, proportion, season, form,
Office, and custom, in all line of order;
          . . . But when the planets
In evil mixture to disorder wander,
What plagues and what portents, what mutiny,
What raging of the sea, shaking of earth,

* regularity of position

Commotion in the winds, frights, changes, horrors,
Divert and crack, rend and deracinate †
The unity and married calm of states
Quite from their fixture! O, when degree is shaked,
Which is the ladder of all high designs,
The enterprise is sick! How could communities,
Degrees in schools, and brotherhoods in cities,
Peaceful commerce from dividable shores,
The primogenitive‡ and due of birth,
Prerogative of age, crowns, sceptres, laurels,
But by degree, stand in authentic place?
Take but degree away, untune that string,
And hark what discord follows! . . .

9 The obedience owed to the Queen

**Lord Burghley's advice to his son, Sir Robert Cecil, was
written after a life spent in her service.**

. . . I do hold, and will always, this course in such matters as I differ in
opinion from her Majesty: as long as I may be allowed to give advice I will
not change my opinion by affirming the contrary, for that were to offend
God, to whom I am sworn first; but as a servant I will obey her Majesty's
commandment and no wise contrary the same, presuming that she being
God's chief minister here, it shall be God's will to have her commandments obeyed; after that I have performed my duty as a councillor,
and shall in my heart wish her commandments to have such good success
as I am sure she intendeth . . .

10 The Queen disobeyed

**When the over-ambitious Dudley was persuaded to accept an
appointment as supreme governor of the Netherlands,
contrary to the Queen's orders, Elizabeth despatched a
stinging letter to him via an envoy.**

How contemptuously we conceive ourself to have been used by you, you
shall by this bearer understand, whom we have expressly sent unto you to
charge you withal. We could never have imagined had we not seen it fall
out in experience that a man raised up by ourself, and extraordinarily

† uproot   ‡ right of the eldest son to succeed to his father's estates

favoured by us above any other subject of this land, would have in so contemptible a sort broken our commandment, in a cause that so greatly toucheth us in honour . . . and, therefore, our express pleasure and commandment is, that all delays and excuses laid apart, you do presently, upon the duty of your allegiance, obey and fulfil whatsoever the bearer hereof shall direct you to do in our name: whereof fail you not, as you will answer the contrary at your uttermost peril.

11 An unfavourable view of the Queen's Council

The Spanish Ambassador reports to King Philip II on the calibre of the Queen's advisers.

. . . The principal person in the Council at present is William Cecil, now Lord Burghley, a knight of the garter. He is a man of mean sort, but very astute, false, lying, and full of all artifice. He is a great heretic and such a clownish Englishman as to believe that all the Christian princes joined together are not able to injure the sovereign of his country . . . and, by means of his vigilance and craftiness, together with his utter un-scrupulousness of word and deed, thinks to outwit the ministers of other princes. This to a certain extent he has hitherto succeeded in doing. Next after him, the man who has most to do with affairs is Robert Dudley, earl of Leicester, not that he is fit for such work, but because of the great favour with which the Queen regards him. He is a light and greedy man who maintains the robbers and lives by their plunder. . . . The other man who has his hand in the government is the Lord Keeper, or guardian, as they call it, of the Great Seal [Sir Nicholas Bacon]. He is an obstinate and most malignant heretic, and, being Cecil's brother-in-law, always agrees with him. The Admiral [the Earl of Lincoln] does not interfere very much in arranging matters, but he is a very shameless thief, without any religion at all, which latter also may be said of the earl of Sussex. . . . There are others of less authority than these men, lawyers, creatures of Cecil, who only repeat what he says. . . .

12 A challenge to the Crown

Peter Wentworth spoke passionately in the 1576 Parliament in favour of freedom of speech and of debate.

Mr Speaker, I find written in a little volume these words in effect: 'Sweet is the name of liberty, but the thing itself a value beyond all inestimable

Queen Elizabeth I receiving Ambassadors

treasure.' So much the more it behoveth us to take care lest we, contenting ourselves with the sweetness of the name, lose and forego the thing, being of the greatest value that can come unto this noble realm. The inestimable treasure is the use of it in this House . . .

. . . I conclude that in this House, which is termed a place of free speech, there is nothing so necessary for the preservation of the prince and state as free speech, and without, it is a scorn and mockery to call it a Parliament House, for in truth it is none, but a very school of flattery and dissimulation, and so a fit place to serve the devil and his angels in, and not to glorify God and benefit the commonwealth. . . .

. . . Amongst other, Mr speaker, two things do great hurt in this place, of the which I do mean to speak. The one is a rumour which runneth about the House, and this it is, 'Take heed what you do; the Queen's Majesty liketh not such a matter; whosoever preferreth it, she will be offended with him': or the contrary, 'Her Majesty liketh of such a matter; whosoever speaketh against it, she will be much offended with him'. The other: sometimes a message is brought into the House, either of commanding or inhibiting, very injurious to the freedom of speech and consultation. I would to God, Mr Speaker, that these two were buried in hell, I mean rumours and messages, for wicked undoubtedly they are . . .

13 The Crown replies to Parliament's challenge

Through her Lord Keeper's address of 1593, Elizabeth reasserted her belief that Parliament's freedom to initiate and debate policy was restricted, and that by implication, the executive power of government lay with the Crown.

. . . her Majesty granteth you liberal but not licentious speech, liberty therefore but with due limitation. For even as there can be no good consultation where all freedom of advice is barred, so will there be no good conclusion where every man may speak what he listeth, without fit observation of persons, matters, times, places and other needful circumstances. It shall be meet therefore that each man of you contain his speech within the bounds of loyalty and good discretion . . . For liberty of speech her Majesty commandeth me to tell you that to say yea or no to bills, God forbid that any man should be restrained or afraid to answer according to his best liking, with some short declaration of his reason therein, and therein to have a free voice, which is the very true liberty of the House; not, as some suppose, to speak there of all causes as him listeth, and to frame a form of religion or a state of government as to their idle brains shall seem meetest. . . .

14 The Queen's Court

Paul Hentzner, a German visitor, was at Greenwich Palace on a Sunday morning in 1598 and watched the splendid sight of the Queen and her attendants as they processed through the hall on their way to the Palace chapel for Sunday service.

First went gentlemen, barons, earls, knights of the Garter, all richly dressed and bareheaded; next came the Lord High Chancellor of England, bearing the seals in a red silk purse, between two, one of whom carried the royal sceptre, the other the sword of state in a red scabbard, studded with golden fleur-de-lis, the point upwards; next came the Queen, in the 65th year of her age (as we were told), very majestic; her face oblong, fair but wrinkled; her eyes small, yet black and pleasant; her nose a little hooked, her lips narrow, and her teeth black (a defect the English seem subject to, from their too great use of sugar); she had in her ears two pearls with very rich drops; her hair was of an auburn colour, but false; upon her head she had a small crown, reported to be made of some of the gold of the celebrated Luneburg table; her bosom was uncovered, as all the English ladies have it till they marry; and she had on a necklace of exceeding fine jewels; her hands were slender, her fingers rather long, and her stature neither tall nor low; her air was stately, her manner of speaking mild and obliging. That day she was dressed in white silk, bordered with pearls of the size of beans, and over it a mantle of black silk shot with silver threads; her train was very long, the end of it borne by a marchioness; instead of a chain, she had an oblong collar of gold and jewels. As she went along in all this state and magnificence, she spoke very graciously, first to one, then to another (whether foreign ministers, or those who attend for different reasons), in English, French and Italian . . . Wherever she turned her face as she was going along, everybody fell down on their knees. The ladies of the court followed next to her, very handsome and well-shaped, and for the most part dressed in white. She was guarded on each side by the gentlemen pensioners, fifty in number, with gilt halberds. In the ante-chapel, next the hall where we were, petitions were presented to her, and she received them most graciously, which occasioned the acclamation of *God save the Queen Elizabeth*! She answered it with *I thank you my good people.*

15 The Queen's jewellery problems

The Queen's Wardrobe Book records the loss of many jewels from her dresses.

Mem(o)., that the 18th of April [1566], her Majesty wore a hat having a band of gold enamelled with knots, and set with twelve small rubies or garnets, at which time one of the said rubies was lost.
Lost from her Majesty's back the 17th of January [1568], at Westminster, one aglet* of gold enamelled blue, set upon a gown of purple velvet, the ground satin; the gown set all over with aglets of two sorts, the aglet which is lost being of the bigger sort.
Item: One pearl and a tassel of gold being lost from her Majesty's back, off the French gown of black satin, the 15th day of July, at Greenwich.
Lost from her Majesty's back, the 14th of May [1579], one small acorn, and one oaken leaf of gold, at Westminster.
Lost by her Majesty, in May [1581], two buttons of gold, like tortoises, with pearls in them, and one pearl more, lost, at the same time, from a tortoise.
Lost at Richmond, the 12th of February, from her Majesty's back, wearing the gown of purple cloth, of silver, one great diamond, out of a clasp of gold, given by the Earl of Leicester. . .
* pendant, or spangle worn on the dress

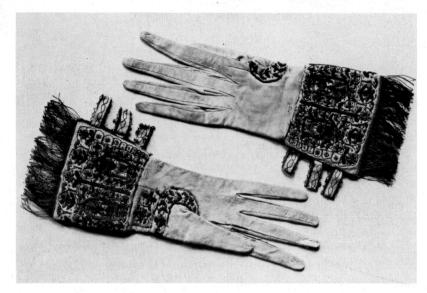

Gloves presented to the Queen on her visit to Oxford University in 1566

16 The Queen's dresses

Some statistics from the Queen's Wardrobe Accounts, 1600, (excluding her Coronation, Mourning and Parliament robes, and those of the Order of the Garter).

Robes	99
French gowns	102
Round gowns	67
Loose gowns	100
Kirtles a skirt or outer petticoat	126
Foreparts stomachers, or ornamental coverings worn under the bodice	136
Petticoats	125
Cloaks	96
Cloaks and safeguards outerskirts, or petticoats worn to protect dresses	91
Safeguards and Jupes women's jackets, kirtles or bodices	43
Doublets	85
Lap mantles	18
Fans	27
Pantofles slippers, or out-door overshoes	9

Queen Elizabeth *c.*1588

POSVI DEVM ADIVTOREM MEVM

SEMPER EADEM

Mars Greenwiciæ
anno Christi
MDXXXIII.
6 Id. Sept.

Virtus erit
MIsericordIæ.

ELISABET D.G. ANGLIAE, FRANCIAE, HIBERNIAE, ET VERGINIAE REGINA,
FIDEI CHRISTIANAE PROPVGNATRIX ACERRIMA. NVNC IN DÑO REQVIESCENS.

17 *The Faerie Queene*
From Book V of Edmund Spenser's poem

They passing by, were guided by degree
Unto the presence of that gracious Queen:
Who sat on high that she might all men see,
And might of all men royally be seen,
Upon a throne of gold full bright and sheen,
Adorned all with gems of endless price,
As either might for wealth have gotten been,
Or could be framed by workman's rare device,
And all embossed with lions and with fleurs-de-lys.

All over her a cloth of state was spread,
Not of rich tissue nor of cloth of gold,
Nor of aught else that may be richest red,
But like a cloud, as likest may be told,
That her broad spreading wings did wide unfold;
Whose skirts were bordered with bright sunny beams,
Glistering like gold, amongst the plights* enrolled,
And here and there shooting forth silver streams,
'Mongst which crept little angels through the glittering gleams.
. . . .

Thus she did sit in sovereign majesty,
Holding a sceptre in her royal hand,
The sacred pledge of peace and clemency,
With which high God had blessed her happy land,
Maugre so many foes which did withstand. †
But at her feet her sword was likewise laid,
Whose long rest rusted the bright steely brand:
Yet when as foes enforced, or friends sought aid,
She could it sternly draw, that all the world dismayed.

* folds   † in spite of the many enemies who opposed her country.

An engraved portrait of Queen Elizabeth

The Queen and marriage

When Elizabeth came to the throne most of her subjects
assumed she would soon marry and that her husband,
whoever he was, would give her invaluable support in tackling
the difficult problems of governing the state. The question of
the Queen's marriage was an issue of national importance for
it was inextricably bound up with safeguarding the succession
to the throne. It was because her position could never be
regarded as secure so long as the succession was in doubt that
Elizabeth's first Parliament strongly urged her to consider
marriage. She answered their petition with an evasive speech
which many must have found surprising for she defended her
choice of a single life and the only comfort she offered to her
anxious listeners was an assurance that if she ever did marry
it would never be to the detriment of the country. She even
ended the speech by predicting the possibility of finishing her
days as a spinster. No one in that 1559 Parliament would have
believed that over forty years later she would die true to her
prophecy.

18   Elizabeth's cautionary words on marriage did not lessen the
hopes of several potential husbands. As a Queen of England,
still in her mid-twenties and endowed with a striking
personality, she presented the most desirable match on the
international marriage market, and soon after her accession
envoys from the unattached kings and princes of Europe
began arriving at the English court to sound out their
masters' prospects. After the ambassador of Philip of Spain
had failed to impress her with the idea of following in the late
Queen Mary's footsteps and linking the destinies of the two
countries again, other suitors from home as well as abroad
tried their luck; but, as William Camden recorded, one man

Queen Elizabeth I in Parliament

19 emerged a clear favourite from the jostle of hopeful lovers.
    Robert Dudley's handsome looks, charming manner and
athletic abilities made him one of the most attractive figures
at Court. There is no doubt the young Queen fell in love with
him and their romance generated the same sort of gossip and
speculation as royal affairs of more recent times. When
Dudley's wife, Amy Robsart, was found dead from a fall in
1560, it was commonly rumoured that the Earl had arranged
her murder to clear the way for his marriage to the Queen.
Elizabeth, however, was left in no doubt that many of her
most trusted advisers, including Cecil, vigorously opposed the
match and that it was unpopular in the country. Dudley was
mistrusted by many, while at Court he had enemies who were
determined to destroy his position and power. There were also
serious political objections to the Queen's choice of a husband
who was one of her courtiers and not of royal blood. It took
Elizabeth a long time to appreciate the impossibility of this
marriage but eventually reason prevailed over emotions and
the relationship settled down into a lasting friendship. The
Queen never lost her deep affection for Dudley whom she
20 liked to call her 'sweet Robin'.
    Many reasons combined to keep Elizabeth unmarried,
especially the apparent impossibility of finding an acceptable
candidate as her royal consort. Political expediency seemed to
rule out an English choice, and religious obstacles excluded
the principal foreign contenders. Personal and psychological
factors were also important. William Camden gave a
21 contemporary's succinct view of the intractable issue.
    Pressure remained on the Queen to marry and was applied
strongly whenever a domestic or foreign crisis occurred. Her
attack of smallpox in 1562, the Northern Rebellion of Catholic
earls in 1569, the growing threat of Spain, and the dangerous
plots centred around Mary, Queen of Scots brought increasing
demands from Parliament for Elizabeth to accept a suitor
and, hopefully, to produce an heir, and thus bring greater
stability to the kingdom.
    The question of her marriage became deeply involved with
foreign policy especially in the 1570s when the balance of
international relationships was upset by Spain's emergence as
the premier power. The Queen used her potential

marriageability as a weapon to secure advantage in the intricate diplomatic manoeuvring that took place amongst the kings and princes of Europe. In 1572 England entered into an anti-Spanish defensive treaty with her traditional enemy, France. The French Queen Mother, Catherine de Medici, who was ambitious for her family's fortunes and wanted to cement the fragile friendship with England, supported the idea of a marriage between her youngest son, the Duke of Alençon and Elizabeth. The negotiations dragged on for nearly ten years, with Elizabeth encouraging Alençon's hopes one moment and dashing them the next. Finally, after innumerable letters and envoys had passed between them, and after visits to England by Alençon and meetings of a commission to settle the marriage terms, Elizabeth allowed the negotiations to peter out. The Duke, who took the title of Anjou in 1574, died in 1584.

Elizabeth's frustrating indecisiveness over the courtship was partly political tactics, motivated mainly by the need to exert a controlling influence on France's ambitions in the Netherlands. There were also critical political and religious obstacles to the match. Elizabeth knew she would lose popular support at home and endanger her throne by marrying a Catholic husband who might become a focus of opposition to her regime. Added to these factors, there was Elizabeth's deep emotional reserve and uncertainty in the matter of close human relationships. Caught in a web of emotional, political and religious tangles, which made inaction seem the only course, Elizabeth was at pains to explain her difficulties to her 'dearest Frog', to keep his hopes alive with fresh declarations of her love, and to absolve herself from the charge of insincere dealing.

22

Elizabeth's relationship with Alençon was no mere flirtation. His ardent and sincere courting genuinely moved her and she responded warmly to his vivacious personality. She was also in her mid-forties and must have realized that it was unlikely another serious suitor would enter her life. The poem she wrote after Alençon's final and inconclusive visit to England reveals her emotional vulnerability, and remains a poignant reminder of the unfulfilled hopes of the Queen's marriage.

23

18 The Queen on marriage, 1559

Elizabeth's first Parliament pleaded with her to consider
marriage for the safety of the country. In her reply, the young
Queen was typically evasive, defending her single life,
reminding members of her 'marriage' to the kingdom (a ploy
which was to become a favourite defensive tactic), and even
foreseeing the possibility of dying as The Virgin Queen.

'Concerning marriage, which you so earnestly move me to, I have been
long since persuaded that I was sent into this world by God to think and
do those things chiefly which may tend to His glory. Hereupon have I
chosen that kind of life which is most free from the troublesome cares of
this world, that I might attend the service of God alone. From which if
either the tendered marriages of most potent Princes, or the danger of
death intended against me, could have removed me, I had long ago
enjoyed the honour of a husband. And these things have I thought upon
when I was a private person. But now that the public care of governing
the kingdom is laid upon me, to draw upon me also the cares of marriage
may seem a point of inconsiderate folly. Yea, to satisfy you, I have already
joined myself in marriage to a husband – namely, the kingdom of
England. And behold, which I marvel you have forgotten, the pledge of
this my wedlock and marriage with my kingdom.' (And therewith she
drew the ring from her finger, and showed it, wherewith at her coronation
she had in a set form of words solemnly given herself in marriage to her
kingdom.) Here having made a pause, she said, 'And do not upbraid me
with miserable lack of children; for every one of you, and as many as are
Englishmen, are children and kinsmen to me; of whom if God deprive me
not, which God forbid, I cannot without injury be accounted barren . . .
Nevertheless if it please God that I enter into another course of life, I
promise you I will do nothing which may be prejudicial to the
Commonwealth, but will take such a husband, as near as may be, as will
have as great a care of the Commonwealth as myself. But if I continue in
this kind of life I have begun, I doubt not but God will so direct my own
and your counsels, that you shall not need to doubt of a successor which
may be more beneficial to the Commonwealth than he which may be born
of me, considering that the issue of the best Princes many times
degenerateth. And to me it shall be a full satisfaction, both for the
memorial of my name, and for my glory also, if, when I shall let my last
breath, it be engraved upon my marble tomb, "Here lies Elizabeth, who
reigned a Virgin and died a Virgin".'

19 The Queen's suitors

Elizabeth's eligibility as a marriage partner attracted a queue
of suitors from home and abroad. The only name missing
from William Camden's following list was Philip of Spain,
who had dropped out of the running at the start of the reign
when Elizabeth had made it clear to his ambassador
that she would not consider marriage to his master.

. . . At the same time there sought to her for marriage Charles, Archduke
of Austria, a younger son of the Emperor Ferdinand; James, Earl of
Arran, commended by the Protestants of Scotland; . . . and Eric, King of
Sweden . . . And at home also there were not lacking some which (as
lovers use to do) feigned unto themselves vain dreams of marrying with
her: namely, Sir William Pickering, Knight, who had some nobility of
birth, a mean estate, but some honour by his studies of good arts,
elegancy of life, and embassies in France and Germany; Henry, Earl
of Arundel, a man of a very ancient nobility, great wealth, but of declin-
ing age; and Robert Dudley, the Duke of Northumberland's younger son
. . . a man of a flourishing age, and comely feature of body and limbs . . .
much favoured by Queen Elizabeth, who heaped honours upon him . . .
Whether this proceeded from any virtue of his, whereof he gave some
shadowed token, or from their common condition of imprisonment under
Queen Mary, or from his nativity, and the hidden consent of the stars at the
hour of their birth . . . a man cannot easily say.

20 The Queen and Robert Dudley

Dudley was perhaps the one real love of Elizabeth's life, and
he retained a special place in the Queen's affections long after
their emotional involvement in the early 1560s. James
Melville, the envoy of Mary, Queen of Scots, recorded two
incidents which reflected the strength of Elizabeth's feelings
for Dudley.

I was required to stay [at court] till I should see him [Dudley] made Earl
of Leicester and Baron of Denbigh; which was done at Westminster with
great solemnity, the Queen herself helping to put on his ceremonial, he
sitting upon his knees before her with a great gravity. But she could not
refrain from putting her hand in his neck, smilingly tickling him, the
French Ambassador and I standing by . . .

Robert Dudley, Earl of Leicester, *c*.1575

She took me to her bed-chamber, and opened a little cabinet, wherein were divers little pictures wrapt within paper, and their names written with her own hand upon the papers. Upon the first that she took up was written, 'My Lord's picture'. I held the candle, and pressed to see that picture so named. She appeared loath to let me see it; yet my importunity prevailed for a sight thereof, and [I] found it to be the Earl of Leicester's picture.

21 Obstacles to the Queen's marriage

In his history of the Queen's reign, William Camden summed up the problems, public and personal, which surrounded the question of a royal marriage.

In the midst of these perplexed cogitations concerning marriage, into which the consideration of the times did necessarily ever and anon cast her, some were of opinion that she was fully resolved in her mind, that she might better provide both for the Commonwealth and her own glory by an unmarried life than by marriage; as foreseeing that if she married a subject, she should disparage herself by the inequality of the match, and give occasion to domestical heartburnings, private grudges and commotions; if a stranger, she then should subject both herself and her people to a foreign yoke and endanger religion: having not forgotten how unhappy the marriage of her sister Queen Mary with King Philip, a foreigner, had been . . . Her glory also, which whilst she continued unmarried she retained entire to herself and uneclipsed, she feared would by marriage be transferred to her husband. And besides, the perils by conception and child-bearing, objected by the physicians and her gentlewomen for some private reasons, did many times run in her mind, and very much deter her from thoughts of marrying.

22 The Queen to Francis, Duke of Alençon

Many love letters passed between Elizabeth and Alençon, with the Queen usually countering the Duke's passionate declarations of love with vague promises. In the following letter of 1579/80, she reminded him that his religion was a stumbling block with the English people, and appeared anxious to clear herself of any charges of insincerity over the marriage negotiations.

I promise you on my faith, that has never yet received spot, that the public exercise of the Roman Religion sticks so in their hearts that I would never consent for you to come among such a company of malcontents . . . I beg you to consider deeply of this, as of a matter which is so hard for Englishmen to bear . . . For my part, I confess that there is no Prince in the world to whom I would more willingly give myself than to yourself, nor to whom I think myself more bound, nor with whom I would pass the years of my life, both for your rare virtues and sweet

Francis,
Duke of Alençon

nature, accompanied with such honourable parts as I cannot recount for number, nor would be so bold to mention for the time that it would needs take. In such wise if you be pleased to consider how that sincerity goes with me in this negotiation, from the beginning until now, I doubt not that I shall appear before the seat of your true judgement to quit me of all subtlety and dissimulation . . . With my commendations to my dearest Frog.

23 The Queen's poem 'On Monsieur's Departure'

Elizabeth is believed to have written this poem after the negotiations had ended with the Duke of Alençon in 1582.

On Monsieur's Departure
I grieve and dare not show my discontent,
  I love and yet am forced to seem to hate,
I do, yet dare not say I ever meant,
  I seem stark mute but inwardly do prate.
    I am and not, I freeze and yet am burned,
    Since from myself another self I turned.

My care is like my shadow in the sun,
  Follows me flying, flies when I pursue it,
Stands and lies by me, doth what I have done.

His too familiar care doth make me rue it.
No means I find to rid him from my breast,
Till by the end of things it be supprest.

Some gentler passion slide into my mind,
For I am soft and made of melting snow;
Or be more cruel, love, and so be kind.
Let me or float or sink, be high or low.
Or let me live with some more sweet content,
Or die and so forget what love ere meant.

Transcript of the letter shown below from Queen Elizabeth I to Sir
Robert Cecil, 1598.
Let the Lordz after their examination sequestar him to his chamber and
Let dru drury be with him til ther doings have bene declared me and that
I Like wel thes warrantz saving that thre be the Lest that suche a
matter deserves and therfor inside of your father that never was with them
the Lord Chamberlain may be incertid who was one for I Like not er in
suche a case.   E.R.

The Queen and religion

Religion has long ceased to have the pervasive influence on people's lives that it exercised in the sixteenth century. In the Elizabethan age the Church was an inseparable part of both public and private life. Attendance at its services was obligatory and whole areas of personal morality and behaviour were subject to its authority. Debate about theological matters was not an academic exercise but often became a passionate issue for the man in the street. Religion could be a disruptive force which divided families and communities, and individuals were liable to be imprisoned or hanged for their faith.

When Elizabeth came to the throne, the country had experienced twenty-five years of religious upheaval. Her father, King Henry VIII, had abolished the Pope's power in England and had become Supreme Head of the Church himself. Although the country remained doctrinally Catholic under Henry, he precipitated the Reformation, and when he was succeeded in 1547 by his young son, King Edward VI, the Church became essentially Protestant in doctrine and practice. When Queen Mary I, a devout Catholic, succeeded Edward in 1553, most of the ecclesiastical changes introduced by Henry and Edward were swept away and Catholicism was restored. In her drive to stamp out Protestant heresy, about three hundred people were burned at the stake in less than five years.

Elizabeth did not share her sister's deeply religious temperament and though she held firm convictions of her own, she pursued a tolerant and unfanatical approach to religious questions. The famous Church Settlement established by Acts of Parliament at the start of her reign was

Queen Elizabeth I at prayer

a compromise solution calculated to be acceptable to as many
Catholics and Protestants as possible, and was designed,
above all, to restore strength and unity to a divided kingdom.
It re-established the Protestant prayer-book of Edward VI but
with alterations which made it more palatable to Catholics,
and it revived Royal Supremacy over the Church, though in a
milder and more parliamentary form than under Henry VIII.
The Settlement survived all manner of vicissitudes, and
provided the conditions from which the Anglican Church has
successfully developed to this day.

A story relating to the early part of the reign tells how the
Queen rebuked the Dean of St Paul's for not clearing his
Cathedral of religious images or pictures which, being
associated with the Catholic past, offended the Queen's
24   Protestant sensibilities and the Church Settlement.

The moderate and broadly-based Church Settlement found
general acceptance during the first decade of the reign,
although like all compromises it did not satisfy the
extremists, whether Catholic or Protestant. Events, however,
upset the relatively harmonious situation. In the late 1560s,
Spain emerged as the leading Catholic power and, with an
army in the Netherlands and a strong navy on the seas,
became an increasing danger to England. At the same time,
Catholicism was being revitalized on the Continent and
missionaries were entering England with the specific purpose
of reconverting the country. A further threat was the arrival
in England of the deposed Mary, Queen of Scots, who
immediately became the focus of Catholic discontent against
the Elizabethan regime. Storm clouds began to gather. In 1569
Elizabeth had to put down a serious rebellion led by the
Catholic Earls of Westmorland and Northumberland. The
next year Pius V issued a Papal Bull of excommunication and
deposition against Elizabeth. Faced with these challenges the
Queen was forced to act, and Parliament passed a series of
severe anti-Catholic measures. The Papal Bull presented a
particularly serious challenge to the regime, and a fearful
dilemma to Catholics, since in absolving all subjects from
their allegiance to the Queen, it forced them to choose
between their religion and their national loyalty, and made
25   them – in the eyes of the government – potential traitors.

At the same time as the Catholic threat intensified, a growing body of reforming Protestants voiced their dissatisfaction with the Elizabethan Church. Most of these Puritans, so called because they wished to 'purify' the Church of all remaining vestiges of Catholicism, accepted the existing structure of the Church and merely demanded an improved standard of clergy and the removal of 'impurities' in doctrine and ritual. Others, however, went much further, attacked the government of the Church by bishops, objected to the Royal Supremacy, and sought a Presbyterian style of Church order.

The Queen's distaste for the Puritan attitude of mind, with its solemn disavowal of the ordinary pleasures of life like music and sports, added fuel to her growing aversion to the political implications of Presbyterian doctrines. In her view, Civil and Church government were two aspects of one state, and the Puritans' refusal to accept the latter, implied opposition to the former. The more radical Puritans, indeed, openly voiced the claim that the final authority in all matters of government lay with the national synod or assembly of the Presbyterian church and that even monarchs were subject to its jurisdiction. Elizabeth spoke her mind on the issue in a letter she wrote to King James VI at a time when Scottish Presbyterians were protecting refugees from England, and publicly praying for their persecuted English brethren.

26 Throughout the mounting religious controversy of her reign, the Queen remained fundamentally concerned with the safety of the kingdom rather than with the theological claims of Protestants or Catholics. The political and not the spiritual import of religion was her prime interest. Since she believed that the essence of religion was deeply personal and that men might come to God by different paths, it was not her wish to pry into individual consciences but only to enforce a degree of outward religious conformity in the interests of national unity. She had an antipathy to religious dogmatists, and is said to have declared that there was 'only one Christ Jesus and one faith; the rest is a dispute about trifles'. When she addressed Parliament in 1585, she declared her opposition both to Catholic agitators and to the 'new-fangleness' of the

27 Puritan extremists.

That there was considerable continuity of tradition despite

Elizabeth receives a book from the poet, George Gascoigne, dedicated to her

the religious changes of the reign is shown by the fact that
many foreign visitors who attended English Church services
were surprised to find how little they differed in form from
the old Catholic rituals. The ceremonies Elizabeth maintained
in her own chapels reflected her innate conservatism about
religion, as with many other matters.

24 The Queen reprimands the Dean of St. Paul's

Elizabeth's aversion to 'Romish relics' is illustrated in the following story which concerns a visit she made to St Paul's Cathedral on New Year's Day, 1561. Alexander Nowell was the unfortunate Dean whose New Year's gift offended Elizabeth's Protestant sensibility.

The Dean, having gotten from a foreigner several fine cuts* and pictures representing the stories and passions of the saints and martyrs, had placed them against the Epistles and Gospels of their festivals in a Common Prayer Book; and this book he had caused to be richly bound and laid on the cushion for the queen's use, in the place where she commonly sat, intending it for a New Year's gift to her majesty, and thinking to have pleased her fancy therewith. But it had not that effect, but the contrary; for she considered how this varied from her late open injunctions and proclamations against the superstitious use of images in churches, and for the taking away all such relics of popery. When she came to her place, she opened the book and perused it, and saw the pictures; but frowned and blushed, and then shut it . . . and, calling the verger, bade him bring her the old book, wherein she was formerly wont to read. After sermon . . . she went straight to the vestry, and applying herself to the Dean, thus she spoke to him:

Queen Mr Dean, how came it to pass that a new service-book was placed on my cushion?

Dean May it please your majesty, I caused it to be placed there.

Queen Wherefore did you so?

Dean To present your majesty with a New Year's gift.

Queen You could never present me with a worse.

Dean Why so, Madam?

Queen You know I have an aversion to idolatry, to images and pictures of this kind.

Dean Wherein is the idolatry, may it please your majesty?

Queen In the cuts resembling angels and saints; nay, grosser absurdities, pictures resembling the Blessed Trinity.

Dean I meant no harm: nor did I think it would offend your majesty when I intended it for a New Year's gift.

Queen You must needs be ignorant then. Have you forgot our proclamation against images, pictures, and Romish relics in the churches? Was it not read in your deanery?

* engravings

Dean   It was read. But be your majesty assured, I meant no harm, when I caused the cuts to be bound with the service-book.

Queen   You must needs be very ignorant to do this after our prohibition of them.

Dean   It being my ignorance, your majesty may the better pardon me.

Queen   I am sorry for it: yet glad to hear it was your ignorance, rather than your opinion.

Dean   Be your majesty assured, it was my ignorance.

Queen   If so, Mr Dean, God grant you his spirit, and more wisdom for the future.

Dean   Amen, I pray God.

Queen   I pray, Mr Dean, how came you to these pictures? Who engraved them?

Dean   I know not who engraved them. I bought them.

Queen   From whom bought you them?

Dean   From a German.

Queen   It is well it was from a stranger. Had it been any of our subjects, we should have questioned the matter. Pray let no more of these mistakes, or of this kind, be committed within the churches of our realm for the future.

Dean   There shall not.

25 The Queen excommunicated and deposed by the Pope

In February 1570, following the Northern Rebellion, Pope Pius V issued a Bull which excommunicated the Queen, deprived her of her title, and released her subjects from their allegiance to her. The vast majority of English Catholics ignored the injunctions, but the threat posed by the Bull forced the government to abandon its lenient policy towards Catholics.

. . . The number of the ungodly has so much grown in power that there is no place left in the world which they have not tried to corrupt with their most wicked doctrines; and among others, Elizabeth, the pretended queen of England and the servant of crime, has assisted in this, with whom as in a sanctuary the most pernicious of all have found refuge. This very woman, having seized the crown and monstrously usurped the place of supreme head of the Church in all England together with the chief authority and jurisdiction belonging to it, has once again reduced this same kingdom –

The conspiracy of the Earls of Northumberland and Westmorland. The execution of Northumberland is shown on the right

The Pope's Bull which excommunicated Queen Elizabeth

Title page of a book published to celebrate the triumph of Elizabeth and James over the enemies of the state (including the Pope, the Armada and Guy Fawkes)

which had already been restored to the Catholic faith and to good fruits – to a miserable ruin. . . .

Therefore, resting upon the authority of Him whose pleasure it was to place us (though unequal to such a burden) upon this supreme justice-seat, we do out of the fullness of our apostolic power declare the foresaid Elizabeth to be a heretic and favourer of heretics, and her adherents in the matters foresaid to have incurred the sentence of excommunication and to be cut off from the unity of the body of Christ.

And moreover (we declare) her to be deprived of her pretended title to the aforesaid crown and of all lordship, dignity and privilege whatsoever.

And also (declare) the nobles, subjects and people of the said realm, and all others who have in any way sworn oaths to her, to be forever absolved from such an oath and from any duty arising from lordship, fealty and obedience; and we do, by authority of these presents, so absolve them and so deprive the same Elizabeth of her pretended title to the crown and all other the abovesaid matters. We charge and command all and singular the nobles, subjects, peoples and others aforesaid that they do not dare obey her orders, mandates and laws. Those who shall act to the contrary we include in the like sentence of excommunication.

26 The Queen to King James VI on the Presbyterians

In this letter, dated July 6, 1590, Elizabeth warned King James of the political dangers posed by the Presbyterians in both their countries. She had learnt that some English Presbyterians had gone to Scotland for aid, and that prayers were being said publicly in some Scottish churches for the persecuted English brethren.

. . . Let me warn you that there is risen, both in your Realm and mine, a sect of perilous consequence, such as would have no Kings but a presbytery, and take our place while they enjoy our privilege . . . Yea, look we well unto them. When they have made in our people's hearts a doubt of our religion, and that we err if they say so, what perilous issue this may make I rather think than mind to write . . . I pray you stop the mouths, or make shorter the tongues, of such ministers as dare presume to make orison in their pulpits for the persecuted in England for the Gospel.

An engraving of one of the attempts to kill Queen Elizabeth, on the *left* officers stopping the assassin, *right* committing suicide in prison

Suppose you, my dear Brother, that I can tolerate such scandals of my sincere government? No. . . . Of this I have particularized more to this bearer, together with other answers to his charge, beseeching you to hear them, and not give more harbour-room to vagabond traitors and seditious inventors, but to return them to me, or banish them your land. And thus with my many thanks for your honourable entertainment of my late embassade, I commit you to God, Who ever preserve you from all evil counsel, and send you grace to follow the best.

Your most assured loving sister and cousin,

ELIZABETH R.

27 The Queen to Parliament on religion

In a speech to Parliament made on March 29, 1585, the Queen made it clear that in her view 'the new-fangleness' of the Puritans was as much a danger to the Church as Catholicism, and that the Puritan doctrines particularly threatened 'kingly rule'.

. . . One matter toucheth me so near as I may not overskip: religion, the ground on which all other matters ought to take root, and being corrupted, may mar all the tree . . .

I see many over-bold with God Almighty, making too many subtle scannings of His blessed will, as lawyers do with human testaments. The presumption is so great as I may not suffer* it. Yet mind I not hereby to animate Romanists (which what adversaries they be to mine estate is sufficiently known) nor tolerate new-fangleness. I mean to guide them both by God's holy true rule. In both parts be perils, and of the latter I must pronounce them dangerous to a kingly rule, to have every man according to his own censure to make a doom of the validity and privity of his prince's government with a common veil and cover of God's word . . .

28 The Elizabethan church service

The French ambassador, de Maisse, visiting England in 1597, was interested to find that the Anglican forms of worship retained many of the elements of the old Catholic services.

As for the manner of their service in church and their prayers, except that they say them in the English tongue, one can still recognise a great part of the Mass, which they have curtailed only in what concerns individual communion, which they only make publicly, and in what is contrary to the doctrine that they hold; for they still keep the Epistle and the Gospel, the *Gloria in Excelsis Deo*, the Creed. They sing the psalms in English, and at certain hours of the day, as at matins and vespers, they use organs and music. The canons wear the amice † and surplice, as also the others, and have copes; and it seems, saving for the images, that there is little difference between their ceremonies and those of the Church of Rome.

* allow   † clerical cap or hood

The Queen and Mary, Queen of Scots

Elizabeth's involvement in the tragic story of Mary, Queen of Scots was perhaps the bitterest experience of her long reign. Mary had been brought up at the French Court and married the Dauphin who became King Francis II in the year following Elizabeth's accession to her throne. Two years later, Mary was forced to return to Scotland after the death of her husband. Mary's arrival posed an obvious threat to Elizabeth and the recently established Protestant settlement in England, for the presence of a staunch Catholic was likely to attract the support of Catholics and to foster the forces of discontent on both sides of the border. Mary was also a great-grand-daughter of Henry VII and therefore an heir apparent to the English throne. Although Elizabeth refused to recognize her cousin's claims to the throne, her policy was to find an acceptable compromise and establish a working relationship between them. She kept on friendly terms with Mary and they wrote affectionate letters to each other, although they never met.

The two queens made a fascinating contrast. Mary was the younger and more attractive woman, and her physical appeal, which led her into three marriages, was a quality which probably aroused some jealousy in the heart of her spinster cousin. Both women were highly educated, shared a gift for languages, and were artistically accomplished. Elizabeth, however, had the greater intellect, and was endowed with two priceless gifts which Mary lacked – political acumen and good judgment of character. That an element of personal rivalry coloured Elizabeth's attitude to her cousin is borne out by the way she quizzed diplomats about the Scottish Queen. James Melville, one of Mary's envoys, responded most adroitly to

Mary, Queen of Scots painted in 1564–5

one of Elizabeth's question sessions, managing to avoid being
29   either disloyal to Mary or discourteous to Elizabeth.

In 1565, Mary married, much to Elizabeth's annoyance,
Henry Stuart, Lord Darnley, another descendant of Henry VII,
who, besides being a claimant after Mary to the English
throne, was a Catholic. Behind Darnley's charming and
handsome facade lurked a man of ruthless ambition and weak
character, and his ill-fated marriage to Mary precipitated a
series of sordid and muddled events which led eventually to
her tragic end. In 1566, seven months after his wedding,
Darnley arranged for Mary's private secretary, David Rizzio,
to be brutally murdered. Obsessed with a desire to be
recognized as King of Scotland in his own right, Darnley had
deeply resented Rizzio's influence over Mary and convinced
himself that the secretary had become her lover. By this time
Scotland was in a state of religious and political turmoil.

Events took another ominous turn less than a year after
Rizzio's assassination when Darnley was murdered. The
suspicion that Mary herself was an accomplice to the crime
mounted to outright condemnation when, within three
months of Darnley's death, Mary was abducted by the Earl of
Bothwell and, after a rigged trial which acquitted Bothwell of
the murder, she married him. Protestants and Catholics alike
were outraged, and the tide turned rapidly against the Queen
and her lover. Bothwell was forced to flee the country, while
Mary was imprisoned and made to abdicate her throne in
favour of James VI, her son by Darnley. In the following year,
1568, Mary escaped and fought one last battle against
Scotland's Protestant forces. She was hopelessly defeated and
fled across the border to England to throw herself on
Elizabeth's mercy.

Elizabeth ordered her unwelcome refugee to be kept in
custody pending an enquiry into her alleged complicity in
Darnley's murder. The results of the hearing were
inconclusive and Mary remained in confinement while her
future was decided. Her arrival in England was a source of
acute embarrassment to Elizabeth. By refusing to renounce
her claims to the English throne, and by being a rallying
figure for Catholics, Mary constituted an obvious danger to
the security of England and the Protestant settlement.

Accordingly, Cecil and other leading ministers wasted no time in advising Elizabeth that as long as Mary remained in England, the country was in danger. Elizabeth, on the other hand, was bound to Mary by family ties and by their identity of interests as queens and anointed sovereigns. Her natural affections and sympathies were also stirred by the touching letters and poems of supplication which Mary sent her.

Against the advice of her ministers, Elizabeth favoured a solution to the problem which would have included Mary's restoration to the Scottish throne, subject to various conditions. However, Elizabeth's plans to reach an amicable arrangement were undermined by Mary's reckless involvement in a series of plots against the English throne, which left her cousin with no option but to extend her exile as a prisoner. In 1571, Mary and the Duke of Norfolk, England's premier nobleman, were implicated in the Ridolfi plot to depose Elizabeth in favour of Mary and to restore Catholicism in England. Parliament and the country at large clamoured for the execution of the two principals. Norfolk went to the block as a traitor and Mary's life was saved only by Elizabeth's refusal to agree to Parliament's demands for her death. Mary learnt no lessons from the experience and continued to conspire against Elizabeth. Finally, in 1586, letters were intercepted from Mary which conclusively proved her involvement in a plot organized by Anthony Babington to murder the English queen and a commission was set up to examine and try Mary at Fotheringhay Castle in Northamptonshire. The stern letter which Elizabeth despatched at the beginning of the trial still reflected her merciful disposition towards her cousin.

The commission, consisting of leading peers, councillors and judges, found Mary guilty on two charges of treason, and in November 1586 both Houses of Parliament unanimously petitioned Elizabeth to proceed to the just sentence of execution. For over two months Elizabeth agonized over the decision. Apart from her abhorrence at the thought of killing a near relative, she was deeply conscious that the execution of an anointed sovereign would strike at the roots of her treasured belief in the divine power of monarchs. She also knew that Mary's death would arouse fierce resentment

throughout Catholic Europe and was likely to spark off
retaliatory action. In her replies to Parliament's demand for
Mary's death, Elizabeth drew on the entire arsenal of her
powers of eloquence to justify her delaying tactics, and
through the moving rhetoric of her speeches can be heard the
note of personal anguish as she prepared to take the most
32   frightful decision of her life.

After endless prevarication, Elizabeth finally gave in to the
insistent demands of her ministers and Parliament. She signed
Mary's death warrant on February 1, 1587, but only after she
had dropped hints that she would prefer a private
assassination to a public execution. These hints were carefully
ignored and Mary went to the block a week later in front of a
crowd at Fotheringhay Castle. She died bravely and
33   unrepentant at the age of forty-four.

Elizabeth was horrified and angered when the news
reached her of Mary's execution. She claimed that although
she had signed the warrant, she had not authorized its
dispatch. In her distraught state she vented her rage on the
entire Council, and in particular on William Davison, her
secretary, whom she had entrusted with the warrant. Davison
was made the scapegoat of the affair and imprisoned in the
Tower. Cynics have interpreted Elizabeth's grief and fury as a
show put on for the sake of her reputation and to ensure that
her alliances with France and with James VI would not be
endangered by Mary's death. But when she wrote to James
expressing her deep sorrow and protesting her innocence,
there is no reason to suppose her feelings were not genuine at
the time, for she had yet to adjust psychologically to the
shattering decision which she, alone, had been forced to
34   make.

29 The Queen inquires about Mary, Queen of Scots

While James Melville was a Scottish envoy at Elizabeth's Court in 1564, he found she was very curious to know details about Queen Mary so that she could compare their respective qualities.

She desired to know of me, what colour of hair was reputed best; and whether my Queen's hair or hers was best; and which of the two was fairest. I answered the fairness of them both was not their worst faults. But she was earnest with me to declare which of them I judged fairest. I said she was the fairest Queen in England, and mine the fairest Queen in Scotland. Yet she appeared earnest. I answered they were both the fairest ladies in their countries; that her Majesty was whiter, but my Queen was very lovely. She inquired which of them was of highest stature. I said, my Queen. 'Then', saith she, 'she is too high; for I myself am neither too high nor too low'. Then she asked what kind of exercises she used. I answered that when I received my dispatch, the Queen was lately come from the Highland hunting: that when her more serious affairs permitted, she was taken up with reading of histories: that sometimes she recreated herself in playing upon the lute and virginals. She asked if she played well. I said reasonably for a Queen . . .

. . . I was stayed two days longer, till I might see her dance, as I was afterward informed. Which being over, she inquired of me, whether she or my Queen danced best. I answered the Queen danced not so high and disposedly as she did.

Then again she wished that she might see the Queen at some convenient place of meeting. I offered to convey her secretly to Scotland by post, clothed like a page; so that under this disguise she might see the Queen . . . telling her that her chamber might be kept in her absence, as though she were sick . . . She appeared to like that kind of language, only answered it with a sigh, saying, 'Alas! if I might do it thus'. She used all the means she could to oblige me to persuade the Queen of the great love she did bear unto her, and that she was fully minded to put away all jealousies and suspicions, and in times coming to entertain a stricter friendship than formerly.

This crayon portrait of Mary was probably made in about 1560

30 Sonnet written by Mary, Queen of Scots, to Queen Elizabeth, 1568

This sonnet was originally composed by Mary in both French and Italian to urge Elizabeth to arrange a meeting between them.

A longing haunts my spirit day and night
Bitter and sweet, torments my aching heart
Between doubt and fear, it holds its wayward part,
And while it lingers, rest and peace take flight.

Dear sister, if these lines too boldly speak
Of my fond wish to see you, 'tis for this –
That I repine and sink in bitterness,
If still denied the favour that I seek.

I have seen a ship freed from control
On the high seas, outside a friendly port,
And what was peaceful change to woe and pain;
Even so am I, a lonely, trembling soul,
Fearing – not you, but to be made the sport
Of Fate, that bursts the closest, strongest chain.

31 The Queen to Mary, Queen of Scots, October 1586

This letter was delivered to Mary at the opening of her trial at Fotheringhay Castle.

You have in various ways and manners attempted to take my life and to bring my kingdom to destruction by bloodshed. I have never proceeded so harshly against you, but have, on the contrary, protected and maintained you like myself. These treasons will be proved to you and all made manifest. Yet it is my will, that you answer the nobles and peers of the kingdom as if I were myself present. I therefore require, charge, and command that you make answer for I have been well informed of your arrogance.

Act plainly without reserve, and you will sooner be able to obtain favour of me.

ELIZABETH

32 The Queen to Parliament on Mary, Queen of Scots, 1586

Following the trial of Mary in October 1586, Parliament petitioned Elizabeth to proceed with the speedy execution of her cousin. On November 12th and on November 24th, delegations from the two Houses attended on the Queen at Richmond to urge her to consent to Mary's death. On both occasions Elizabeth replied with emotional speeches in which she played for time and deferred her decision.

. . . as I came to the crown with the willing hearts of subjects, so do I now, after twenty-eight years' reign, perceive in you no diminution of good wills, which, if haply I should want, well might I breathe but never think I lived. . . . I protest it is and hath been my grievous thought that one, not different in sex, of like estate, and my near kin, should be fallen into so great a crime. Yea, I had so little purpose to pursue her with any colour of malice, that as it is not unknown to some of my Lords here – for now I will play the blab – I secretly wrote her a letter upon the discovery of sundry treasons, that if she would confess them, and privately acknowledge them by her letters unto myself, she never should need be called for them into so public question . . .

And if, even yet, now the matter is made but too apparent, I thought she truly would repent – as perhaps she would easily appear in outward show to do – and that for her none other would take the matter upon them; or that we were but as two milk-maids, with pails upon our arms; or that there were no more dependency upon us, but mine own life were only in danger, and not the whole estate of your religion and well doings; I protest . . . I would most willingly pardon and remit this offence . . . for we Princes, I tell you, are set on stages, in the sight and view of all the world duly observed. The eyes of many behold our actions; a spot is soon spied in our garments, a blemish quickly noted in our doings. It behoveth us, therefore, to be careful that our proceedings be just and honourable.

And since now it is resolved that my surety cannot be established without a Princess's head, I have just cause to complain that I, who have in my time pardoned so many rebels, winked at so many treasons, and either not produced them or altogether slipped them over with silence, should now be forced to this proceeding, against such a person. I have besides, during my reign, seen and heard many opprobrious books and

Pen and ink sketch of the trial of Mary, Queen of Scots at Fotheringhay
Castle, October 14–15 1586. She is seated on the right (A)

pamphlets against me, my Realm and State, accusing me to be a tyrant. I thank them for their alms. I believe therein their meaning was to tell me news: and news it is to me indeed. I would it were as strange to hear of their impiety. What will they not now say, when it shall be spread that for the safety of her life a maiden Queen could be content to spill the blood even of her own kinswoman? I may therefore full well complain that any man should think me given to cruelty; whereof I am so guiltless and innocent as I should slander God if I should say He gave me so vile a mind. Yea, I protest, I am so far from it that for mine own life I would not touch her . . .

33 The execution of Mary, Queen of Scots, 1587

Robert Wyngfield gave Lord Burghley a detailed eye witness account of the execution of Mary which took place in the Great Hall of Fotheringhay Castle on the morning of February 8, 1587.

. . . The said eighth day of February being come, and time and place appointed for the execution, the said Queen being of stature tall, of body corpulent, round-shouldered, her face fat and broad, double-chinned, and hazel-eyed, her borrowed hair aborn*, her attire was this. On her head she had a dressing of lawn edged with bone lace, a pomander chain and an *Agnus Dei* about her neck, a Crucifix in her hand, a pair of beads at her girdle, with a silver cross at the end of them. A veil of lawn † fastened to her caul‡ bowed out with wire, and edged round about with bone lace. Her gown was of black satin painted, with a train and long sleeves to the ground . . .

Then, with an unappalled countenance, without any terror of the place, the persons, or the preparations, she came out of the entry into the hall, stepped up to the scaffold, being two foot high and twelve foot broad, with rails round about, hanged and covered with black, with a low stool, long fair cushion, and a block covered also with black. The stool brought her, she sat down . . . [and] began very fastly with tears and a loud voice to pray in Latin, and in the midst of her prayers, with overmuch weeping and mourning, slipped off her stool, and kneeling presently said divers other Latin prayers . . .

Then she began to kiss her crucifix, and to cross herself, saying these words, 'Even as thy arms, oh Jesu Christ, were spread here upon the cross,

---

* i.e. she was wearing her wig   † fine linen   ‡ a netted cap

The execution of Mary, Queen of Scots at Fotheringhay Castle, February 8 1587. The sketch shows three stages: the entry of the Queen on the left, her preparation, and her execution

so receive me into the arms of mercy'. Then the two executioners kneeled down unto her, desiring her to forgive them her death. She answered, 'I forgive you with all my heart. For I hope this death shall give an end to all my troubles'. They, with her two women helping, began to disrobe her.

During the disrobing of this Queen, she never altered her countenance, but smiling said she never had such grooms before to make her unready, nor ever did put off her clothes before such a company. At length unattired and unapparelled to her petticoat and kirtle, the two women burst out into a great and pitiful shrieking, crying, and lamentation, crossed themselves, and prayed in Latin. The Queen turned towards them . . . crossed and kissed them, and bade them pray for her, and not to be so mournful, for (said she) this day I trust shall end your Mistress' troubles.

Then with a smiling countenance she turned herself to her menservants, Melvin and the rest, standing upon a bench near unto the scaffold, who were sometimes weeping and sometimes crying out aloud, and continually crossing themselves, and prayed in Latin. And the said Queen (thus turned unto them) did herself likewise cross them and bid them farewell and prayed . . .

This done one of her women having a Corpus Christi cloth lapped it up three-corner wise and kissed it and put it over the face of her Queen and Mistress, and pinned fast on the caul of her head . . . Then she laid herself upon the block most quietly, and stretching out her arms and legs cried out 'In manus tuas, Domine' etc. three or four times. At last while one of the executioners held her straightly with one of his hands, the other gave two strokes with an axe before he did cut off her head, and yet left a little gristle behind. At which time she made very small noise and stirred not any part of herself from the place where she laid.

Then the executioner which cut off her head lifted it up and bade God save the Queen; then her dressing of lawn fell from her head which appeared as grey as if she had been three score and ten years old, pulled very short, her face being in a moment so much altered from the form which she had when she was alive, as a few could remember her by her dead face; her lips stirred up and down almost a quarter of an hour after her head was cut off.

Then said Mr Deane so perish all the Queen's enemies. And afterwards the Earl of Kent came to the dead body and, standing over it, with a loud voice likewise said, such end happen to all the Queen's and the Gospel's enemies.

Then one of the executioners pulling off her garters espied her little dog which was under her clothes, which could not be gotten forth but by force and afterwards would not depart from her dead corpse, but came and laid between her head and shoulders . . .

34 The Queen to King James VI, 1587

This letter, dated February 14, 1587, was written shortly after the Queen had been shocked at receiving the news of the execution of Mary, Queen of Scots.

My dear Brother,

I would you knew (though not felt) the extreme dolour that overwhelms my mind, for that miserable accident which (far contrary to my meaning) hath befallen. I have now sent this kinsman of mine, whom ere now it hath pleased you to favour, to instruct you truly of that which is too irksome for my pen to tell you. I beseech you that as God and many more know, how innocent I am in this case: so you will believe me, that if I had bid aught I would have bid by it. I am not so base minded that fear of any living creature or Prince should make me afraid to do that were just; or done, to deny the same. . . . Thus assuring yourself of me, that as I know this was deserved, yet if I had meant it I would never lay it on others' shoulders; no more will I not damnify myself that thought it not.

The circumstance it may please you to have of this bearer. And for your part, think you have not in the world a more loving kinswoman, nor a more dear friend than myself; nor any that will watch more carefully to preserve you and your estate. And who shall otherwise persuade you, judge them more partial to others than you. And thus in haste I leave to trouble you: beseeching God to send you a long reign . . .

Your most assured loving sister and cousin,

ELIZABETH R.

The defeat of the Spanish Armada

England's relations with Spain deteriorated throughout the 1580s. There was growing hostility at sea between the two countries, reflected in the mounting number of incidents in home waters and around the coasts of the New World. There was evidence of Spanish involvement in plots against Elizabeth, culminating in 1584 when the Spanish Ambassador was expelled from the country for being implicated in a plan to release Mary, Queen of Scots, and overthrow Elizabeth. There was increasing conflict in the Low Countries, resulting in Elizabeth's decision in 1585 to send an army into the Netherlands to oppose the Spanish forces. Finally, the execution of Mary, Queen of Scots, brought open war one stage closer.

The crisis came to a head with Philip II's decision to prepare a fleet which would sail up the English Channel, rendezvous with a flotilla carrying Spanish troops from the Netherlands under the command of the Duke of Parma, and prepare the way for an invasion of England. The Spanish king had been assured that English Catholics would rise in support of his invading army; the Pope gave his moral support and promised massive financial aid once the army had landed; and there was French backing for the enterprise from Henry of Guise.

The impending confrontation was viewed with intense expectancy, and there was a widespread feeling that the result would not only determine the future of Protestant England but would be decisive for the whole of Europe. A messianic fervour was in the air, with both sides regarding the conflict in terms of a holy war. On May 28, 1588, the Spanish fleet of one hundred and thirty ships, bearing two thousand four hundred guns and thirty thousand men, put out from Lisbon,

under the command of the Duke of Medina-Sidonia. The
great enterprise, however, began inauspiciously, for the fleet
was soon battered by bad storms and was forced into
Corunna to refit and revictual. The delay gave the English
valuable time to strengthen their defences and make final
preparations. Under the supervision of John Hawkins,
the English navy had been equipped with a new kind of ship,
lighter and more versatile than the heavy Spanish galleons,
35 and armed with superior long-range guns.

On July 21 the two fleets engaged in action off the
Eddystone and for a week there was a running battle up the
Channel. Lord Howard of Effingham in the 'Ark Royal'
commanded the English fleet, with Francis Drake acting as
his Vice-Admiral aboard 'The Revenge', and there were
seamen of the calibre of John Hawkins and Martin Frobisher
in charge of squadrons. Misunderstandings delayed the
planned rendezvous between Parma's troops and Medina-
Sidonia's ships, and while the Armada anchored indecisively
off Calais, Howard sent in fireships. Forced to scatter and
subjected to heavy English bombardment, the Armada tried
36 to escape into the North Sea and to return home by sailing
37 around Scotland and past the Irish coast.

Meanwhile, during the final stages of the conflict in the
Channel, Elizabeth went to Tilbury on the River Thames where
an English army had been assembled by Leicester in
readiness to repel any invasion by Parma's troops. Dressed in
white velvet and carrying a gold and silver truncheon, the
Queen rode down the ranks and inspected her soldiers. Later
there was a review and march past, and the Queen addressed
38 her famous and stirring words to the troops.

The storms encountered by the Armada ships as they fled
north on their long route back to Spain inflicted worse damage
than they had suffered from English guns. Altogether the
enterprise was a disastrous setback for Spain. About a third of
the fighting ships were lost and many of the surviving
vessels that limped back were severely damaged. Less than
five thousand of the eighteen thousand soldiers who had
embarked from Spain returned. Although the result of the
battle did not decide the issue of war between England and
Spain, it was a turning-point in English and European history.

This medal was struck
to commemorate the defeat
of the Armada

The threat to Elizabeth's throne and the future of
Protestantism was lifted, at least for the immediate future,
and for Spain the military and psychological setback marked
the beginning of its decline as an imperial power. In England,
the defeat of the Armada released an extraordinary outburst
of national rejoicing and instilled a new sense of patriotic
pride and confidence which affected many areas of life. The
glory of the hour was reflected on the Queen in particular and
helped to foster her image as a dazzling and divinely-inspired
ruler, feared by her enemies and loved by her subjects. Her
extraordinary success was, indeed, acknowledged by her
adversaries. Pope Sixtus V admitted 'she certainly is a great
Queen and were she only a Catholic she would be our dearly
beloved. Just look how well she governs! She is only a woman,
only mistress of half an island, and yet she makes herself
feared by Spain, by France, by the Empire, by all'. Elizabeth's
own countrymen fully endorsed the Pope's sentiments about
their queen's supremacy.

39

35 The Armada battle

The chronicler and antiquarian John Stow (*c.* 1525–1605) included an account of the defeat of the Armada in his famous history book, *The Annals of England.*

The Spanish navy having refreshed themselves, after 28 days rest, set forward for England about the 11th of July, in the greatest pomp that ever eye beheld, matchless in state, commanding their passage wheresoever they came . . .

The 19th of July, the English Admiral upon direct knowledge of the enemies' approach, sends speedy summons unto all the English fleet . . . The 21st of July the Spaniards came as high as Plymouth where divers English ships lay fast in harbour; the rest gave charge upon the enemy. The Armado then deraigns* itself into the fashion of the crescent moon; each side prepares themselves speedily to fight with braves and bravadoes, their shrill sounding trumpets and their rattling drums lend mutual courage unto both battle lines and loud thundering cannons send swift messengers of death. Both armies strive to get advantage of the wind but the English, being much more quick and yare †, win their desire, and England's Admiral, in person, gave the on-set and for two hours space maintained a valiant fight until night drew on . . .

The next day the English navy being well increased gave charge and chase upon the enemy, squadron after squadron, seconding each other like swift horsemen, that could nimbly come and go and fetch the wind for most advantage. Now begins the furious fight on either part . . . Both navies showed great valour in their daily fight, which commonly continued within the reach of musket shot and many times at push of pike, without intermission, save only when, through want of wind, they were restrained. The English chieftains ever sought to single out the great Commanders of the Spanish host whose lofty castles held great scorn of their encounter; but while both armies were thus conjoined, Don Pedro de Valdes, a chief commander of the Army, fell foul upon one of his fellows and broke his foremast, who, being maimed and left behind, lay like a stiff elephant in the open field beset with eager hounds; who being commanded to yield said he would yield to none but to his equal, and asked in whose squadron he was fallen. They answered into Drake's squadron . . . whereupon he yielded.

* arrays   † prepared

36 Sir Francis Drake to Sir Francis Walsingham, July 31, 1588

Sir Francis Drake wrote to the Queen's Secretary, Sir Francis Walsingham, from his Armada ship, requesting that his Spanish prisoners, including Don Pedro de Valdes, be delivered up to the Queen personally.

Most Honourable,

I am commanded to send these prisoners ashore by my lord-admiral . . . Let me beseech your honour that they may be presented unto her Majesty, either by your honour or my honourable good lord my lord-chancellor, or both of ye. Their Don Pedro is a man of great estimation with the King of Spain, and thought next in his army to the Duke of Sidonia. That they should be given from me unto any other, it would be some grief to my friends. If her majesty will have them, God defend but I should think it happy. We have the army of Spain before us, and mind, with the grace of God, to wrestle a fall with them. There was never any thing pleased me better than the seeing the enemy flying with a south wind to the northward . . . With the grace of God, if we live, I doubt it not but, ere it be long, so to handle the matter with the Duke of Sidonia as he shall wish himself at St Marie among his orange trees. God give us grace to depend upon Him, so shall we not doubt victory, for our cause is good.

Humbly taking my leave, this last of July 1588, your honour's faithfully to be commanded ever, FRA. DRAKE.

P.S. I crave pardon of your honour for my haste, for that I had to watch this last night upon the enemy.

37 The defeat of the Armada

From John Stow's *The Annals of England*

The Spanish navy for 5 days space having endured many sharp fights and fierce assaults . . . the seven and twentieth of July towards night they cast anchor near to Calais Road, the English likewise rid anchor very near unto them. Now rides the Armado at her wished port, unto whom the Duke of Parma sends present word that within 3 days their forces would conjoin, and with first advantage of wind and tide, transport their armies to the English coast . . .

Sir Francis Drake

Whilst this lusty navy like a demi-conqueror rid thus at anchor, the Spanish faction in sundry nations had divulged that England was subdued, the Queen taken and sent prisoner over the Alps to Rome, where barefoot she should make her humble reconciliation.

In Paris, Don Barnardino de Mendoza, Ambassador from Spain, entered into our Lady Church, advancing his rapier in his right hand, and with a loud voice cried 'Victory, victory' and it was forthwith bruited that England was vanquished. But the next day when the truth was known of the Armado's overthrow . . . Mendoza, being much dismayed, obscured himself, not daring to show his face . . .

The English forces being now wholly united, prevented their enemies conjoining together and followed their fortunes to the uttermost, continuing four days fight in more deadly manner than at any time before and, having incessant cause of fresh encouragement, chased the Spaniards from place to place, until they had driven them into a desperate state . . . In whose pursuit . . . when they saw them past the Orkneys and the Scottish seas, the English made retreat . . .

The Queen upon certain knowledge of the Spaniards coming, forthwith settled all her land forces in warlike readiness . . . She went in person to Tilbury where her presence and princely encouragement Bellona*-like, infused a second spirit of love, loyalty and resolution into every soldier in her army . . .

38 The Queen's Armada speech

Elizabeth's famous words were spoken to her troops at Tilbury on August 9, 1588, when, as a contemporary wrote, 'full of princely resolution and more than feminine courage . . . she passed like some Amazonian empress through all her army'.

My loving people, we have been persuaded by some that are careful of our safety, to take heed how we commit ourselves to armed multitudes, for fear of treachery. But I assure you, I do not desire to live in distrust of my faithful and loving people.

Let tyrants fear! I have always so behaved myself that, under God, I have placed my chiefest strength and safeguard in the loyal hearts and good will of my subjects; and therefore I am come amongst you, as you see, at this time, not for my recreation and disport, but being resolved, in the midst and heat of the battle, to live or die amongst you all, and to lay down for my God, for my kingdom, and for my people, my honour and my blood, even in the dust.

I know I have the body of a weak and feeble woman, but I have the heart and stomach of a king, and of a king of England too, and think foul scorn that Parma or Spain, or any prince of Europe, should dare to invade the borders of my realm; to which, rather than any dishonour shall grow by me, I myself will take up arms, I myself will be your general, judge, and rewarder of every one of your virtues in the field.

I know already, for your forwardness you have deserved rewards and crowns †; and we do assure you on the word of a prince, they shall be duly paid you. In the meantime, my Lieutenant-General‡ shall be in my stead,

* Goddess of War   † the coin worth five shillings   ‡ Robert Dudley

than whom never prince commanded a more noble or worthy subject; not doubting but that by your obedience to my general, by your concord in the camp, and by your valour in the field, we shall shortly have a famous victory over these enemies of my God, my kingdom, and of my people.

39 The Queen's reputation abroad

In his book *The History of Great Britaine*, published in 1611, John Speed praised the success of Elizabeth's foreign policies. Although his account seems excessively eulogistic, it does genuinely reflect the extraordinary international reputation that the Queen won for herself.

. . . The great affairs of Europe mainly depended upon her directions, who sitting at the helm of the ship . . . arbitrated and guided their estates both in peace and war: *Spain*, seeking to overflow all, was beaten back and scarcely able to maintain her own banks: In *France* the house of Valois [was] under-propped by her counsel; that of Bourbon, advanced by her countenance, forces and treasure; *Scotland* relieved by her love; *Netherlands* by her power; *Portugal's* King by her bounty; *Poland* by her commiseration; likewise *Germany*, *Denmark*, *Sweden*, often took up and laid down arms at her beck and dispose. Neither could the utmost bounds of Europe (the *Russians* and *Tartars*) contain the limits and extent of her great fame; but that the same pierced further into the remoter parts of *Asia*, *Africa*, *America*, among the *Turks*, . . . among the *Persians*, *Barbarians*, *Indians*, and where not.

The Queen at leisure

Elizabeth's strong sense of her public responsibilities led her
always to give first priority to the affairs of state. Edmund
Bohun wrote, 'In her private way of living, she always
preferred her necessary affairs and the despatch of what
concerned the government, before and above any pleasures,
recreations and conversation'. But the Queen's dedication to
her duties and her exceptional capacity for the hard work of
administration were matched with a zest for enjoying her
leisure hours. She knew how to set aside her burdens of office
and join her friends and her subjects in the common pastimes
of the age. She was aware, too, that keeping a balance between
work and recreation, study and exercise, was a sound recipe
for mental and physical health. She herself enjoyed
remarkably good health until the last years of her life and
was able to sustain her indefatigable stamina for dealing with
the day-to-day affairs of government. Her secret lay mainly in
taking daily exercise and observing a careful diet. Although
40 her Royal Household consumed vast quantities of food, she
41 herself ate and drank very little.

Meals at Court were great social occasions and their serving
was accompanied by elaborate rituals, but Elizabeth
preferred to eat simply and alone in her private apartments,
away from the chatter and laughter of the palace dining
42 hall.

Music and dancing were favourite recreations. It was said of
her life at Richmond Palace that 'six or seven galliards of a
morning, besides musics and singing, were her ordinary
exercise'. She was an accomplished musician, playing both the
virginals and the lute, and she could sing and compose.
Ambassadors sometimes arrived to find her playing music,

and on one occasion she entertained one of her suitors, Archduke Charles of Austria, by playing her lute to him on board a boat on the Thames. She was very fond of dancing
43 throughout her life and was able to display her skill in a
44 coranto only a few weeks before her final illness.

There are many contemporary reports of the Queen's love of riding and hunting. She regularly rode ten miles or more a day until the last months of her life, and never lost her interest in the chase. In September 1600 she was, despite her advanced years, 'excellently disposed to hunting, for every second day she is on horseback and continues the sport long'. She spent much time riding, for, apart from the days passed in the countryside, she often processed on horseback through the streets of London, or inspected her army from the saddle, or rode during the course of her famous progresses. These latter were the tours she conducted through the counties of southern England and the midlands during many summers of the reign. Although the progresses were pleasurable excursions in themselves, during which the Queen was lavishly entertained and fêted, they also carried considerable propaganda value in enabling Elizabeth to make contact with her subjects and impress her authority on them. As a contemporary noted wisely, 'In pompous ceremonies a secret of government doth much consist', and there is no doubt that the journeys of the royal cortège through the towns and countryside of her kingdom were a highly effective public relations exercise on behalf of the monarchy. The Spanish ambassador was one of many who witnessed the rapturous reception given to
45 Elizabeth on her progresses.

Since the Queen was accompanied on progress by many members of her Court, her entourage would number two or three hundred. The journeys were made in short stages, usually from one nobleman's great house to the next. Planning the tours and making all the necessary practical arrangements was an administrative headache which mainly
46 devolved on the Lord Chamberlain.

Wherever the Queen went on progress, a variety of ceremonies and entertainments was devised in her honour, with speeches, bell-ringing, concerts, theatrical spectacles, feasts, dancing and hunting amongst the staple ingredients of the programmes. In 1572 she visited Warwick and stayed at the Castle as the guest of the Earl, Ambrose Dudley. On her entry into the town she was met by the principal citizens, including the Recorder who delivered a speech of welcome in which, having confessed to feeling rather overwhelmed by his responsibility, he proceeded to talk at some length of the Queen's wise government, and then gave her a short history of Warwick. As so often on these occasions when she came into direct contact with her ordinary subjects, the Queen displayed her marvellous instinct for the right word and gesture to seal an affectionate relationship between herself and her people. She called the Recorder to her, offered her hand to him to kiss, smiled and said, 'Come hither, little Recorder. It was told me that you would be afraid to look upon me or to speak so boldly, but you were not so afraid of me as I was of you, and I now thank you for putting me in mind of my duty'. It was moments such as this which so endeared her to the nation. A few days after this incident the Queen was treated to a firework display which did not quite go according to plan and her 'common touch' of humanity was again made

47   evident.

The Elizabethan aristocrats vied with each other in offering lavish hospitality to the Queen on her progresses. The basic costs of a visit were paid by the Royal Household itself but many of the wealthier courtiers chose to make a grand social display of a royal visit, and paid handsomely for the privilege of welcoming the Queen to their houses. A ten-day visit to Lord Burghley in 1591 cost over £1000, and Robert Dudley spent several thousands of pounds when she stayed for nearly three weeks at Kenilworth Castle in 1575. Even a modest one-day visit to a courtier became a carefully staged and expensive operation for him.

48   The Queen was keenly interested in theatre and did much to support and encourage the acting profession at a time when English drama was developing into greatness. She inherited the traditional court interlude players but in 1583 she formed a company of professional actors known as Queen Elizabeth's Men, consisting of twelve of the finest players in the country, whose performances dominated the theatre world for many years. The Queen's company often travelled into the

provinces during the summer months and gave performances
in various towns, including Stratford-upon-Avon where a
young man called William Shakespeare probably saw them.
The nobility often responded to the Queen's love of theatre by
49   arranging performances of plays and masques when she
50   visited them.

The entertainments devised for the Queen were not always
sophisticated or lavish spectacles. Some of the more
memorable incidents during her progresses happened when
countryfolk offered her a simple welcome or an unpretentious
gift, as an old shepherd did when she visited Sudeley Castle in
1592. Seeing the unhurried and relatively untroubled life of a
rustic labourer, the Queen must sometimes have sympathised
with the words spoken by her ancestor King Henry VI in
51   Shakespeare's play, who longed to exchange the anxieties and
52   stress of his public office for the countryman's existence.

Elizabeth carried in procession by her courtiers in 1601. Although the queen
was ageing she still realized the importance of public appearances

40 The food consumption of the Queen's Household

Average annual consumption of the Royal Household under Queen Elizabeth.

600,000	gallons of beer
300	tons of wine
1,240	oxen
8,200	sheep
13,260	lambs
2,700	dozen chickens and capons
60,000	pounds of butter
4,200,000	eggs

41 The Queen's eating habits

Sir John Clapham recorded that in contrast to some members of her Household, Elizabeth was abstemious over food and drink.

The Queen was in her diet very temperate, as eating but few kinds of meat and those not compounded*. The wine she drank was mingled with water, containing three parts more in quantity than the wine itself. Precise hours of refection she observed not, as never eating but when her appetite required it.

42 The Queen dines

Thomas Platter, a Swiss tourist, visited Nonsuch Palace in 1599 and observed the elaborate preparations for the Queen's dinner.

Now when the queen had returned to her chamber, her guardsmen wearing tabards, red, if I remember, with the royal arms on their backs embroidered in gold, carried two tables into the room with trestles, and set them down where the queen had been sitting. Then another two entered each bearing a mace and bowed three times; first at their entrance, and by the door, then in the centre of the room and lastly in front of the table, and after they had laid it they withdrew again. Soon two

* i.e. elaborately prepared

Queen Elizabeth on her way to Nonsuch Palace, 1582

more guards in tabards appeared bowing with plates and other things which they laid on the table. Following them came another two bowing, and placed the carving-knives, bread and salt upon the table. Then a gentleman bearing a mace entered, together with a charming gentle-woman or lady-in-waiting, who bowed very gracefully, as described above, thrice to the empty table, at the same time a gentleman with a mace arrived with another gentleman and all four stood before the table.

Then straightway came the queen's guardsmen with red tabards folded back, one behind the other, and if I am not mistaken, a weapon at their sides, each one bearing a single covered dish of food. They are all very tall, fine, strong men, and all similarly attired, so that I never in my life saw their like. I believe there must have been forty of them.

When they had handed over the food a gentleman removed the cover, while the lady-in-waiting served and carved a large piece off, which she gave to the guard who had carried it in, and who was supposed to eat the portion, though they generally took it out or merely tasted a morsel.

Two of them brought wine and beer which was also poured out and tasted. And after this long table had been fully laid and served and the same obeisance and honours performed as if the queen herself had sat

Elizabeth playing the lute
by Nicholas Hilliard, c.1580

there, whatever dishes there were, were offered to the queen in her
apartment for her to make her choice. These were sent into her and she
ate of what she fancied, privily however, for she very seldom partakes
before strangers, and the remainder was carried out again to the lords'
table; and the guards brought other fresh dishes, which were served like
the former, and I observed amongst them some very large joints of beef,
and all kinds of game, pasties and tarts. After the third course had been
thus brought in, served and removed again, and the dessert prepared and
cleared off, the queen's musicians appeared in the presence chamber with
their trumpets and shawms*, and after they had performed their music,
everyone withdrew, bowing themselves out just as they had come in, and
the tables were carried away again.

43 The Queen plays the virginals

**James Melville, the Scottish ambassador, was impressed by
Elizabeth's musicianship.**

That same day after dinner my Lord of Hunsdon drew me up to a quiet
gallery . . . where I might hear the Queen play upon the virginals. After I

* an early kind of oboe

had hearkened a while, I took by the tapestry that hung before the door of the chamber, and seeing her back was toward the door, I entered within the chamber, and stood a pretty space hearing her play excellently well. But she left off immediately, so soon as she turned her about and saw me. She appeared to be surprised to see me, and came forward, seeming to strike me with her hand; alleging she used not to play before men, but when she was solitary, to shun melancholy. She asked how I came there. I answered, 'As I was walking with my Lord of Hunsdon, as we passed by the chamber-door, I heard such melody as ravished me, whereby I was drawn in ere I knew how'; excusing my fault of homeliness, as being brought up in the Court of France, where such freedom was allowed . . .

44 The Queen's dancing skills

The French ambassador, writing in 1597, noted the Queen's love of dancing.

She takes great pleasure in dancing and music. She told me that she entertained at least sixty musicians; in her youth she danced very well, and composed measures and music, and had played them herself and danced them. She takes such pleasure in it that when her Maids dance she follows the cadence with her head, hand and foot. She rebukes them if they do not dance to her liking, and without doubt she is a mistress of the art, having learnt in the Italian manner to dance high.

45 The Queen on Progress

The Spanish ambassador described the Queen's reception during her progress in 1568.

She was received everywhere with great acclamations and signs of joy, as is customary in this country; whereat she was extremely pleased and told me so, giving me to understand how beloved she was by her subjects and how highly she esteemed this, together with the fact that they were peaceful and contented, whilst her neighbours on all sides are in such trouble. She attributed it all to God's miraculous goodness. She ordered her carriage sometimes to be taken where the crowd seemed thickest, and stood up and thanked the people.

46 Planning the Queen's Progress, 1591

In this letter the Lord Chamberlain, Lord Hunsdon, who was responsible for making all the practical arrangements for the Queen's progress, wrote to Sir William More about a forthcoming visit of Elizabeth's to southern England. The tour seems to have caused some trouble to the Chamberlain.

. . . I have thought good to let you understand that her Majesty is resolved to make a Progress this year as far as Portsmouth, and to begin the same the 22 or 23 of this month, and to come to your house. She is very desirous to go to Petworth and Cowdray, if it be possible; but none of us all can set her down any where to lie at between your house and Cowdray. And therefore I am to require you that you will set this bearer some way for her to pass, and that you will let some one of your own men who is best acquainted with that way, to be his guide, that he may see whether they be fit for her Majesty or no. And whether it will be best going from your house to Petworth, and so to Cowdray, or else from your house to Cowdray. And if you can set her down [at] any place between your house and Cowdray that may serve her for one night, you shall do her a great pleasure, and she will take it very thankfully at your hands. But I have thought good to let you understand that, though she cannot pass by Cowdray and Petworth, yet she will assuredly come to your house, and so towards Portsmouth such other way as shall be set down to her . . . And so I commit you to God. In haste, July 10, 1591, your very loving friend,
HUNSDON.

47 The Queen's visit to Warwick, 1572

The entertainment devised for Elizabeth on her visit to Warwick included a spectacular firework display and mock battle which did not pass off without unfortunate results.

Her Majesty that Saturday night was lodged again in the Castle at Warwick; where also she rested all Sunday; where it pleased her to have the country people, resorting to see the dance in the court of the Castle, her Majesty beholding them out of her chamber window, which thing, as it pleased well the country people, so it seemed her Majesty was much delighted, and made very merry. That afternoon passed, and supper done, a show of fireworks [was] prepared for that purpose in the Temple fields . . .

Queen Elizabeth at a hunting picnic

Queen Elizabeth enthroned on the left, enjoying the water sports during her visit to Elvetham, Hampshire in 1591

There was devised on the Temple ditch a fort made of slender timber covered with canvas. In this fort were appointed divers persons to serve as soldiers, and therefore so many harnesses as might be gotten within town were had, wherewith men were armed [and] appointed to show themselves; some others [were] appointed to cast out fireworks, as squibs and balls of fire. Against that fort was another castle prepared of like strength whereof was governor, the Earl of Oxford, a lusty gentleman, with a lusty band of gentlemen. Between these forts or against them were placed certain battering-pieces, to the number of twelve or thirteen, brought from London, and twelve score chambers or mortar-pieces, brought also from the town, at the charge of the Earl of Warwick. These pieces and chambers were by trains fired, and so made a great noise as though it had been a sore assault; having some intermission in which time the Earl of Oxford and his soldiers to the number of two hundred with calivers and harquebuses* likewise gave divers assaults; [they in] the fort [began] shooting again and casting out divers fires, terrible to those that have not been in like experience, valiant to such as delighted therein and indeed strange to them that understood it not, for the wild fire falling into the River of Avon would for a time lie still and then again rise and fly abroad casting forth many flashes and flames; whereat the Queen's

* early types of portable guns

Majesty took great pleasure; till after, by mischance, a poor man or two were much troubled; for at the last, when it was appointed that the overthrowing of the fort should be, a dragon, flying, casting out huge flames and squibs, lighted upon the fort, and so set fire thereon . . . But whether by negligence or otherwise, it happened that a ball of fire fell on a house at the end of the bridge, wherein one Henry Cowy, otherwise called Miller, dwelt, and set fire on the same house, the man and wife being both in bed and in sleep, which burned so, as before any rescue could be, the house and all things in it utterly perished, with much ado to save the man and woman; . . . And no marvel it was that so little harm was done, for the fire-balls and squibs cast up did quite fly over the castle, and into the midst of the town . . .

This fire appeased, it was time to go to rest; and in the next morning it pleased her Majesty to have the poor old man and woman that had their house burnt brought unto her; whom so brought, her Majesty comforted very much, and, by her great bounty, and other courtiers, there was given toward their losses that had taken hurt, £25.12s.8d. or thereabouts . . .

48 The Queen visits Sir Robert Sidney

Sir Robert Sidney described, in a letter to a friend, a day's visit paid to his house by the Queen, probably in 1600 when she was in her late sixties.

Her Highness hath done honour to my poor house by visiting me, and seemed much pleased at what we did to please her. My son made her a fair speech, to which she did give most gracious reply. The women did dance before her, whilst the cornets did salute from the gallery; and she did vouchsafe to eat two morsels of rich comfit cake, and drank a small cordial from a gold cup. She had a marvelous suit of velvet borne by four of her first women attendants in rich apparel; two ushers did go before, and at going up stairs she called for a staff, and was much wearied in walking about the house, and said she wished to come another day. Six drums and six trumpets waited in the court, and sounded at her approach and departure. My wife did bear herself in wondrous good liking, and was attired in a purple kirtle, fringed with gold; and myself, in a rich band and collar of needlework, and did wear a goodly stuff of the bravest cut and fashion, with an under body of silver and loops. The Queen was much in commendation of our appearances, and smiled at the ladies, who in their dances often came up to the step on which the seat was fixed to make their

obeisance, and so fell back into their order again. The younger Markham*
did several gallant feats on a horse before the gate, leaping down and
kissing his sword, then mounting swiftly on the saddle, and passed a lance
with much skill. The day well nigh spent, the Queen went and tasted a
small beverage that was set out in divers rooms where she might pass; and
then in much order was attended to her palace, the cornets and trumpets
sounding through the streets.

49 The Queen's theatre company

In March 1583 Edmund Tilney, Master of the Revels, was
ordered 'to choose out a companie of players for her Maiestie'.
As Stow's *Annals* recorded, twelve talented actors were picked
to form the company known as Queen Elizabeth's Men.

Comedians and stage-players of former time were very poor and ignorant
in respect of these of this time: but being now grown very skilful and
exquisite actors for all matters, they were entertained into the service of
divers great lords: out of which companies there were twelve of the best
chosen, and, at the request of Sir Francis Walsingham, they were sworn
the queen's servants and were allowed wages and liveries as grooms of the
chamber: and until this year 1583, the queen had no players. Among
these twelve players were two rare men, viz. Thomas Wilson, for a quick,
delicate, refined, extemporal wit, and Richard Tarleton, for a wondrous
plentiful pleasant extemporal wit, he was the wonder of his time.

50 The Queen enjoys theatre

In 1564 when Elizabeth was the guest of Sir Richard Sackville,
a comedy and a masque were arranged in her honour. The
Spanish ambassador, Diego de Silva, described the scene.

After supper . . . the Queen came out to the hall, which was lit with many
torches, where the comedy was represented. I should not have
understood much of it, if the Queen had not interpreted, as she told me
she would do. They generally deal with marriage in the comedies . . .
The comedy ended, and then there was a masque of certain gentlemen
who entered dressed in black and white, which the Queen told me were
her colours, and after dancing a while one of them approached and
handed the Queen a sonnet in English, praising her.

* Gervase Markham, a noted horseman

The guests at a wedding feast being entertained by actors and musicians

A few months later the same ambassador witnessed the
performance of a comedy before the Queen at Court. The
play dealt again with the topical subject of marriage.

The plot was founded on the question of marriage, discussed between
Juno and Diana, Juno advocating marriage and Diana chastity. Jupiter
gave a verdict in favour of matrimony, after many things had passed on
both sides in defence of the respective arguments. The Queen turned to
me and said, 'This is all against me'. After the comedy there was a
masquerade of Satyrs, or wild gods, who danced with the ladies, and
when this was finished there entered 10 parties of 12 gentlemen each, the
same who fought in the foot tourney, and these, all armed as they were,
danced with the ladies; a very novel ball, surely.

51 A Cotswold shepherd addresses the Queen

This speech was addressed to the Queen by an old shepherd
when she entered Sudeley Castle in 1592.

Vouchsafe to hear a simple shepherd; shepherds and simplicity cannot
part. Your Highness is come into Cotswold, an uneven country, but a
people that carry their thoughts level with their fortunes; low spirits, but
true hearts; using plain dealing, once counted a jewel, now beggary.
These hills afford nothing but cottages, and nothing can we present to
your Highness but shepherds. The country healthy and harmless, a fresh
air, where there are no damps, and where a black sheep is a perilous beast;
no monsters; we carry our hearts at our tongues' ends, being as far from
dissembling as our sheep from fierceness; and if in anything we shall
chance to discover our lewdness, it will be in over-boldness, in gazing at
you, who fills our hearts with joy and our eyes with wonder . . .

This lock of wool, Cotswold's best fruit, and my poor gift, I offer to
your Highness, in which nothing is to be esteemed but the whiteness,
virginity's colour; nor to be expected but duty, shepherd's religion.

52 Royal thoughts on the shepherd's life

From *King Henry VI, Part 3*, Act 2, scene 5, by William
Shakespeare

O God! methinks it were a happy life
To be no better than a homely swain;

To sit upon a hill, as I do now,
To carve out dials quaintly*, point by point,
Thereby to see the minutes how they run –
How many makes the hour full complete,
How many hours brings about the day,
How many days will finish up the year,
How many years a mortal man may live.
When this is known, then to divide the times –
So many hours must I tend my flock;
So many hours must I take my rest;
So many hours must I contemplate;
So many hours must I sport myself;
So many days my ewes have been with young;
So many weeks ere the poor fools will ean †;
So many years ere I shall shear the fleece:
So minutes, hours, days, weeks, months, and years,
Pass'd over to the end they were created,
Would bring white hairs unto a quiet grave.
Ah, what a life were this! how sweet! how lovely!
Gives not the hawthorn bush a sweeter shade
To shepherds looking on their silly sheep,
Than doth a rich embroider'd canopy
To kings that fear their subjects' treachery?
O yes, it doth; a thousand-fold it doth.
And to conclude, the shepherd's homely curds,
His cold thin drink out of his leather bottle,
His wonted sleep under a fresh tree's shade,
All which secure and sweetly he enjoys,
Is far beyond a prince's delicates –
His viands sparkling in a golden cup,
His body couched in a curious‡ bed,
When Care, Mistrust, and Treason waits on him.

---

* i.e. to carve sundials ingeniously (perhaps in the turf)   † yean, or to bring forth (lambs)

‡ elaborately carved

Treason: the Essex rebellion

The Queen's final years were sad and troublesome, and no darker shadow fell across them than the abortive attempt of the young Earl of Essex to seize power. Essex pushed his way to favour at Court after the deaths of some of Elizabeth's oldest friends and most trusted advisers. His own stepfather, the Earl of Leicester, died in 1588, leaving the Queen grief-stricken at the loss. Within the next few years many other of Elizabeth's long-serving councillors died, including Sir Walter Mildmay, Sir Francis Walsingham, Sir Christopher Hatton and Sir Francis Knollys. Into the vacuum left by these elder statesmen stepped a new generation of power-seeking courtiers, the most ambitious of whom was Robert Devereux, Earl of Essex.

At first the Queen was much attracted to the handsome and gifted stepson of her old favourite, Robert Dudley, and a special relationship developed between them. She was thirty-four years older than the Earl but the gap seemed negligible in
53 the face of the young man's irresistible charms and flattery.

The relationship, however, was a precarious one, for Elizabeth was soon aware that, despite Essex's many qualities, there was a reckless and potentially dangerous element in his character. In 1589 he disobeyed her orders and left Court to sail in an expedition commanded by Sir Francis Drake. Two years later he acted bravely but irresponsibly when he was commanding an English army in Normandy. Returning from his military adventures, the Earl determined to seek political power and gathered behind him a formidable following of young courtiers and army captains who shared a common frustration with establishment politics. Their main opponent was the Cecil faction led by the ageing Lord Burghley and his younger son, Robert, who had been carefully trained and prepared for political office by his father and who inherited many of the great stateman's gifts.

The Queen kept a close watch on the growing rivalry between the Essex and Cecil parties in the 1590s and sought to maintain a balance between them so that she could control the situation. With a lifetime of political experience behind her, she knew the risk of giving too much power to the Earl, a man who, in the French ambassador's words, 'in no wise contents himself with a petty fortune and aspires to greatness'. Although she continued to grant honours to her favourite, Elizabeth shrewdly made sure that all the key political appointments which fell vacant were filled by men who were not Essex supporters.

The Earl's political ambitions were checked but he soon increased his popular support by resuming his role as a valiant soldier and leading the Cadiz expedition of 1596 which sacked the town and caused the destruction of the Spanish West Indies fleet. Three years later he seized another chance to play the military hero – this time with fatal results. By the end of 1598 the Queen was faced with a major crisis in Ireland where control of most of the country had been wrested from the English occupation forces by the Spanish-backed Earl of Tyrone. A huge army was assembled to fight the Irish rebels, and after bringing relentless pressure to bear on the Queen and the Council, Essex secured his appointment as Lord Deputy of Ireland and commander of the troops. Full of confidence and hope, he left England at the head of his army in March 1599.

Essex arrived in Ireland with detailed instructions regarding the type of campaign he was to fight. From the start he blindly disregarded his orders, wasted men and time on minor engagements, and then, to the Queen's indignation, ended seven futile and costly months of campaigning by arranging a truce with Tyrone. Faced with his terrible failure the Earl blamed enemies at home and talked recklessly of returning with his army and marching on London. Instead he broke his orders of command in a milder manner, left for England with a handful of friends, and, reaching Nonsuch Palace, threw himself on the Queen's mercy.

Within hours Essex was under arrest. It was the end of his career, though not yet of his life. After confessing his faults, he was spared a state trial and went before a commission of councillors and judges. He was suspended from all his offices and confined to his own home at the Queen's pleasure. From

56   his imprisonment in Essex House he wrote despairingly to her.

In August 1600 the Earl was set free but banned from Court. Despite his resolve to spend the rest of his life in retirement, he was soon complaining bitterly about his treatment and dropping dark hints about reasserting his power. His paranoia intensified on learning that in addition to his political ruin he faced bankruptcy, and in a state of distress and depression he became convinced he had been made a victim of a deliberate

57   and vindictive campaign.

Encouraged by his supporters, many of whom were, like himself, disillusioned and penniless, Essex was persuaded to attempt an armed rebellion which would raise the City of London against the Court, and force the Queen to institute changes in government. After the rising he expected positions in Court and government to be filled by his adherents, while he would be elevated to high office. The rebellion was launched on February 8, 1601, but the militia and populace of London failed to rise in his support and the revolt was a fiasco. By the end of the day the conspirators were in

58   custody.

Eleven days after his attempted coup d'état, Essex stood trial in Westminster Hall before twenty-five peers and was found guilty of treason. The Queen showed leniency and spared the lives of all except six of the rebels. The Earl was one of those condemned to die. Although she was much affected by his downfall, revoking his death warrant once, the same inexorable logic that had forced her hand against Mary, Queen of Scots, made Essex's execution inevitable. As Elizabeth herself bluntly said, 'Those who touch the sceptres of princes deserve no pity'. Essex had destroyed himself at the

59   age of thirty-four.

Robert
Devereux,
Second Earl
of Essex

53 The Earl of Essex to Queen Elizabeth, 1591

This flattering letter was written by Essex from Normandy
where he was commanding an English army sent to support
Henry of Navarre.

Most fair, most dear, and most excellent Sovereign . . . The two
windows of your Privy Chamber shall be the poles of my sphere,
where, as long as your Majesty will please to have me, I am fixed

and unmovable. When your Majesty thinks that heaven too good for me, I will not fall like a star, but be consumed like a vapour by the sun that drew me up to such a height. While your Majesty gives me leave to say I love you, my fortune is as my affection, unmatchable. If ever you deny me that liberty, you may end my life, but never shake my constancy, for were the sweetness of your nature turned into the greatest bitterness that could be, it is not in your power, as great a Queen as you are, to make me love you less.

54 Essex's departure for Ireland, March 1599

Essex left for Ireland at the head of 16,000 footsoldiers and 1,300 horsemen, the largest army raised during the Queen's reign. John Stow recorded that the sudden change in the weather which occurred during the Earl's departure was taken by some people as a bad omen.

The 27th of March 1599, about two o'clock in the afternoon, Robert Earl of Essex, Vicegerent of Ireland, took horse in Seeding Lane, and from thence being accompanied with divers noblemen and many others, himself very plainly attired, rode through Grace Street, Cornhill, Cheapside, and other high streets, in all which places and in the fields the people pressed exceedingly to behold him, especially in the highways for more than four miles space, crying and saying 'God bless your Lordship, God preserve your honour', and some followed him until the evening only to behold him. When he and his company came forth of London the sky was very calm and clear; but before he could get past Islington, there arose a great black cloud in the north-east, and suddenly came lightning and thunder, with a great shower of hail and rain; the which some held as an ominous prodigy.

55 Essex's return to England, September 1599

Essex abandoned his command in Ireland on September 24, 1599, and after a four-day journey, ending with a frantic ride to Nonsuch Palace, he burst into the Queen's bedroom to explain his actions and the failure of his campaign. Rowland Whyte witnessed his arrival and Elizabeth's reaction to it.

Nonsuch, Michaelmas Day, 1599

On Michaelmas Eve, about 10 o'clock in the morning, Lord Essex

An engraving of the Earl of Essex

lighted at Court Gate Post, made all haste up to the Presence, and so to the Privy Chamber, and stayed not till he came to the Queen's Bedchamber, where he found the Queen, newly up, her hair about her face; he kneeled unto her, kissed her hands, and had some private speech with her, which seemed to give him great contentment; for coming from her Majesty to go shift himself* in his chamber, he was very pleasant, and thanked God that, though he had suffered much troubles and storms

* i.e. to change his clothes

abroad, he found a sweet calm at home. 'Tis much wondered at here that he went so boldly to her Majesty's presence, she not being ready, and he so full of dirt and mire, that his very face was full of it. When ready he went up again for half an hour after twelve. As yet all was well, and her usage very gracious towards him.

But when, after dinner, he again went into her presence, he found her much changed, for she began to call him to question for his return, and was not satisfied in the manner of his coming away and leaving all things at so great hazard. She appointed the lords to hear him, and so they went to Council in the afternoon. It is mistrustful that for his disobedience he shall be committed. On the same evening a commandment came from the Queen to my Lord of Essex, that he should keep his chamber.

56 The Earl of Essex to the Queen, May 12, 1600

After his return from Ireland, Essex was kept under arrest but the Queen tempered his imprisonment by allowing him to be confined to his own house. He found himself the subject of various tracts and speeches, and knew that his name was being bandied about in the taverns. Convinced he was being libelled by his enemies, and helpless to defend himself, he wrote the following desperate letter to the Queen.

. . . Now that the length of my troubles and the increase of your indignation have made all men so afraid of me as my own poor state is ruined, and my friends and servants like to die in prison, because I cannot help myself with my own, I not only feel the weight of your indignation, and am subject to their malicious informations that first envied me your favour, and now hate me out of custom; but, as if I were thrown into a corner like a dead carcase, I am gnawed on and torn by the basest creatures upon earth. The prating tavern haunter speaks of me what he lists; the frantic libeller writes of me what he lists; they print me and make me speak to the world, and shortly they will play me upon the stage.

The least of these is worse than death, but this is not the worst of my destiny; for you, who have protected from scorn and infamy all to whom you once avowed favour but Essex, and never repented of any gracious assurance you had given till now, have now, in this eighth month of my close imprisonment, rejected my letters, and refused to hear of me, which to traitors you never did. What remains is only to beseech you to conclude my punishment, my misery and my life, altogether, that I may go to my

Saviour, who has paid himself a ransom for me, and whom (me thinks) I still hear calling me out of this unkind world, in which I have lived too long, and once thought myself too happy.

57 The Earl of Essex insults the Queen

From Camden's *Annals*

The Earl of Essex in the meanwhile kept at home, and . . . now and then he let fall some words which showed his disdainful stomaching [of] the power his adversaries had with the Queen; in which those that loved him best judged there was more passion than discretion . . . These things coming to the Queen's knowledge alienated her affection from him more and more: but the affront he did her in undervaluing her personal shape inflamed her most of all. For he had given out, (to mention nothing else) that being now an old woman, she was no less crooked and distorted in mind than she was in body . . .

Hearkening to evil counsellors, he began secretly to hammer anew those clandestine designs he was formerly upon in Ireland, for the removing of his enemies forcibly from the Court. Fresh projects every day offered themselves to him, and there wanted not such as would put them in execution.

58 The Essex Rebellion, 1601

John Stow described the events in London on February 8, 1601, when Essex rode into the city with a company of two to three hundred men and tried, with disastrous results, to persuade 'the general multitude' to join them in seizing the Court, the Tower, and the City.

Sunday the 8th of February 1601, the Earl of Essex, upon advice of his friends, came to London about ten o'clock, assisted with the chief gallants of the time, viz. the Earl of Southampton, Sir Charles Danvers, Sir Christopher Blount, Robert Catesby, and many others; and as they passed Fleet Street, cried 'For the Queen; for the Queen' . . . The general multitude, being entirely affected to the Earl, said that the Queen and the Earl were made friends, and that her Majesty had appointed him to ride in that triumphant manner through London, unto his house in Seeding Lane, and all the way he went, the people cried, 'God save your Honour, God bless your Honour'.

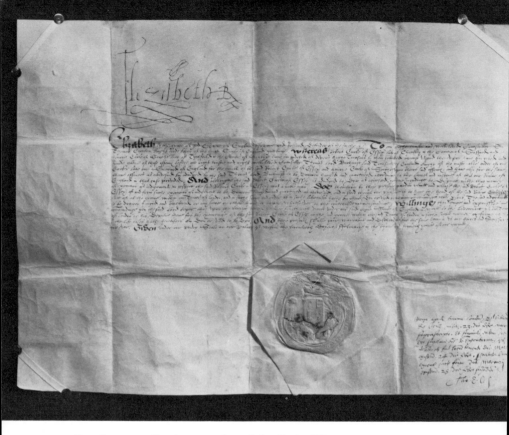

Royal warrant for the execution of the Earl of Essex

The Lord Mayor, being at Paul's Cross, received warning from the Council to look to the City, and by eleven of the clock the gates were shut and strongly guarded. The Earl kept his course towards Fenchurch and entered into Master Thomas Smith's house, Sheriff of London, where the Earl drank; in which space the Sheriff went out at a back door unto the Lord Mayor, offering his service, and requiring direction. The Earl went into an armourer's house, requiring munition, which was denied him: from thence the Earl went to and fro, and then came back to Gracechurch Street, by which time the Lord Burghley was come thither, having there in the Queen's name, proclaimed the Earl and all his company traitors, as he had done before in Cheapside.

At hearing whereof, one of the Earl's followers shot a pistol at the Lord Burghley; whereupon he well perceiving the stout resolution of the Earl's followers, together with the people's great unwillingness either to apprehend the Earl or aid him, returned to the Court; assuring the Queen, that notwithstanding the great love the Londoners bare unto the Earl, yet they will not aid him: the Court being now fortified and double guarded, the streets in divers places set full of empty carts and coaches, to stop the Earl's passage, if he should attempt to come that way . . .

About two of the clock, the Earl having passed to and fro through divers streets, and being forsaken of divers his gallant followers, he resolved to make his nearest way home; and coming towards Ludgate, he was strongly resisted by divers companies of well-armed men, levied and placed there by the Lord Bishop of London; then he retired thence, Sir Christopher Blount being taken and sore wounded in the head; from thence the Earl went into Friday Street and being faint, desired drink, which was given him; and at his request unto the citizens, the great chain which crosseth the street was held up to give him passage; after that he took boat at Queenshithe, and so came to his house . . . (and) fortified his house with full purpose to die in his own defence. But when he beheld the great artillery, and the Queen's forces round about the house, being sore vexed with the cries of ladies, about ten of the clock at night he yielded himself unto the Lord Admiral, earnestly desiring his trial to be speedy and honourable, which was performed.

59 The trial and execution of the Earl of Essex
From the accounts of John Stow and William Camden

The 19th of February, the Earl of Essex and the Earl of Southampton were arraigned at Westminster: they were jointly and severally indicted. The chief points were for holding of private counsels and conspiring to deprive the Queen of life and government . . . The prisoners were found guilty, and the sentence of death was denounced against them . . . The news of all this day's business was suddenly divulged throughout London; whereat many forsook their suppers, and ran hastily into the streets to see the Earl of Essex as he returned to the Tower, who went a swift pace, bending his face towards the earth, and would not look upon any of them, though some spake directly to him.

The Queen in the meantime wavered in her mind concerning him. On the one side, her former affection and favour towards him recalled her to some degree of clemency, and she sent her command that he should not be executed: on the other side, his perverse obstinacy, who scorned to ask her pardon, and had declared openly that his life would be the Queen's destruction, did so prick her forward to use severity, that shortly after she sent a fresh command that he should be put to death . . .

The final years

The failure of Essex to win support for his rebellion, and the
effective way it was handled, gave the Queen greater authority
than ever before. 'She could put forth such altercations when
obedience was lacking as left no doubtings whose daughter
she was', commented her godson, Sir John Harington. Cast in
her father's mould, she retained her commanding control over
the country's affairs until the end of her life. Yet the Queen
was shaken and dispirited by the Essex tragedy. She had been
forced to execute a man of great talent whose company she
had enjoyed for over a decade. Furthermore, she was aware
that Essex's challenge to the government had been backed by
gifted members of the younger generation of courtiers. Her
state of mind was described by Harington when he visited the
60   court in the aftermath of the Essex rising.
The cause of the Queen's distress was not only Essex's
death but also her awareness of the onset of old age. She had
outlived the friends and companions of her own generation,
and was beginning to feel the erosion of the skills and vigour
which had sustained her authority and indomitable spirit for
so long. She fought bravely against her physical decline,
continuing to take regular exercise. She concealed the
discomforting effects of rheumatism in her hands and made
light of neuralgic pains in her face caused by decayed teeth.
She refused to abandon her summer progresses and was
furious when Lord Hunsdon suggested it was unwise for 'one
of her years' to ride from Hampton to Nonsuch Palace. She
tried desperately to maintain a youthful appearance by
resorting to cosmetics, huge wigs, and bejewelled clothes.
These helped to preserve the illusion of an ageless monarch
on public occasions but close to, as the French ambassador

61 discovered, these externals disguised a less attractive reality.
After reigning so long, and with such evident success,
through a period of momentous change, the Queen became a
legendary figure in her own lifetime. In the popular
imagination she seemed a superhuman being, and courtiers
and poets addressed her as though she were a goddess. The
notion of the monarch endowed with semi-divine qualities
was encouraged by Elizabeth herself who believed
passionately in preserving the mystique of kingship. Her
unmarried state, which was a political liability, was cleverly
turned into a cult of the Virgin Queen and became a kind of
emotional substitute for the old reverence accorded to the
Virgin Mary. The myth, however, of the Virgin Queen married
in spirit to her whole kingdom and not in body to any one
person, was sustained at a personal cost which the Queen
seemed to recognize. Her poem 'When I was fair and young',
probably written at the time of the Essex tragedy, poignantly
62 reveals the lonely woman behind the facade of monarchy.[62]

The Essex rising was not an isolated incident which ruffled
an otherwise peaceful close to the reign. The Queen's final
years were troubled ones, with the mood of the country being
more sombre and uncertain than at any time since her
accession. Her avowed intention to avoid the horror of war
and its ruinous cost to the nation was thwarted. English
armies became deeply involved in the Netherlands and in
Ireland, and the kingdom was drawn into open conflict with
Spain at sea. By the end of the century the huge military
expenditure had created a financial crisis which forced the
Queen to sell off her own lands and the country to suffer
heavy taxation. Domestic issues aggravated the strains of war.
Unemployment, inflation and food shortages became serious
problems in the 1590s and led to mounting parliamentary
criticism of the whole system of government finance.

The Queen's last Parliament, held in the autumn of 1601
when the country was drifting towards bankruptcy, proved to
be a stormy one. Financial grievances dominated the debates,
with members being especially resentful of the Crown's use of
monopolies, or grants giving exclusive rights to an individual
to market a commodity. The licensing of all production under
grants was regarded by the Queen as a traditional part of her

royal prerogative and therefore stood above criticism. But merchants and businessmen saw monopolies as harmful to free enterprise and an unwarrantable interference in the economic rights of the individual. It had also become obvious to them that monopolies were no longer given as genuine incentives to commercial entrepreneurs but had degenerated into a system of rewards for Court favourites and a means of securing political patronage. Faced with an explosive issue which raised constitutional as well as economic matters, the Queen gave way to the Commons's demands and promised to reform the monopolies system. It was a face-saving act designed to prevent her royal prerogative being made the subject of open debate but, as usual with Elizabeth, it was achieved with political artistry. After she had informed the Commons of her decision to rescind the monopolies practice, she invited a deputation of members to attend her at Whitehall Palace and delivered her famous 'Golden Speech' to

63   them.

Sixteen months after her memorable speech the Queen was dead. By the end of 1602 it was clear her powers were failing and she had become the victim of bouts of melancholia and insomnia. A contemporary noted that 'she sleepeth not so much by day as she used, neither taketh rest at night. Her delight is to sit in the dark, and sometimes with shedding tears to bewail Essex'. A ray of sunshine pierced the gloom when news arrived from Ireland that Essex's successor, Lord Mountjoy, had crushed Tyrone's revolt, but her decline continued its inevitable course. In February 1603 the gold ring she had worn since her coronation had to be cut from her

64   swollen finger. Its removal symbolized the end of her
65   marriage to her subjects.

The Queen is said to have ordered all the mirrors in her private rooms to be taken away so that she did not have to be reminded of the ravages of old age. A contemporary also recorded that at the very end of her life she commanded a looking-glass to be brought to her. She was shocked to see her wrinkled face, and expressed anger at the courtiers who had continued to flatter her. In Shakespeare's play *Richard II* the deposed King is also brought a mirror and seeing his reflection, comments bitterly on the illusion of majesty.

Earlier in the play he had let slip his kingly mask and
revealed the vulnerable figure dressed in the robes of
authority. That the story of Richard's deposition was a highly
sensitive political subject is made clear by the Essex
conspirators' choice of Shakespeare's play for propagandist
revival on the eve of their rebellion. The Queen herself later
66 admitted that theatre audiences identified the character of the
67 King with her.

Before she died Elizabeth probably broke her lifetime's
silence on the subject of her successor by indicating that
James VI of Scotland should follow her. In any case she was
aware that Robert Cecil had been making all the necessary
arrangements for a smooth transfer of power to the Scottish
king. It was, however, religious matters and not political
questions which occupied Elizabeth's thoughts during her
last days. Her mind was on the next world and not on things
of this earth when she died on March 24, 1603, in her
68 seventieth year.

The Queen's funeral was an impressive and moving
ceremony, in which over a thousand mourners dressed in
hoods and suits of black formed the procession. As the hearse
moved slowly through the streets of London bearing the coffin
to Westminster Abbey for burial, the weeping crowds felt that
an era had come to an end. Before long some of those who
lined the route would refer nostalgically to Elizabeth's time as
a golden age. As her reign receded further into the past, it
became more certain that she had presided over and helped to
shape one of the most creative and colourful chapters in
England's history. And since her remarkable personality was
indelibly stamped on her times, future generations gave her
69 own name to the period she lived through, and acclaimed the
70 Elizabethan age.

60 Sir John Harington to Sir Hugh Portman, 1601

The Queen's godson described the mood of the Queen shortly after the Essex conspiracy. Harington had been one of many knights created by Essex in Ireland, and his association with the Earl still rankled with Elizabeth.

My Honoured Friend,

. . . For six weeks I left my oxen and sheep, and ventured to Court, where I find many leankinded beasts, and some not unhorned. Much was my comfort in being well received, notwithstanding it is an ill hour for seeing the queen. The madcaps are all in riot, and much evil threatened. In good sooth I feared her majesty more than the rebel Tyrone, and wished I had never received my Lord of Essex's honour of knighthood. She is quite disfavoured, and unattired, and these troubles waste her much. She disregardeth every costly cover* that cometh to the table, and taketh little but manchet † and succory pottage‡. Every new message from the City does disturb her, and she frowns on all the ladies. I had a sharp message from her brought by my Lord Buckhurst, namely thus, 'Go tell that witty fellow, my godson, to get home; it is no season now to fool it here'. I liked this as little as she doth my knighthood, so took to my boots and returned to the plough in bad weather. I must not say much, even by this trusty and sure messenger; but the many evil plots and designs have overcome all her highness' sweet temper. She walks much in her privy chamber, and stamps with her feet at ill news, and thrusts her rusty sword at times into the arras in great rage. My Lord Buckhurst is much with her, and few else since the city business; but the dangers are over, and yet she always keeps a sword by her table. . . . (I) will not leave my poor castle of Kelston, for fear of finding a worse elsewhere, as others have done. I will eat Aldborne rabbits, and get fish (as you recommend) from the man at Curry-Rival; and get partridge and hares when I can, and my venison where I can; and leave all great matters to those that like them better than myself . . .

---

* i.e. dish   † wheat-bread   ‡ chicory soup

61 The Queen in her mid-sixties

Sieur de Maisse, an envoy from France, spent some months in 1597–98 in England, and wrote of the Queen and her court.

She was strangely attired in a dress of silver cloth, white and crimson, or silver 'gauze', as they call it. This dress had slashed sleeves lined with red taffeta, and was girt about with other little sleeves that hung down to the ground, which she was for ever twisting and untwisting. She kept the front of her dress open, and one could see the whole of her bosom, and passing low, and often she would open the front of this robe with her hands as if she was too hot. The collar of the robe was very high, and the lining of the inner part all adorned with little pendants of rubies and pearls, very many, but quite small. She had also a chain of rubies and pearls about her neck. On her head she wore a garland of the same material and beneath it a great reddish-coloured wig, with a great number of spangles of gold and silver, and hanging down over her forehead some pearls, but of no great worth. On either side of her ears hung two great curls of hair, almost down to her shoulders and within the collar of her robe, spangled as the top of her head. Her bosom is somewhat wrinkled as well as (one can see for) the collar that she wears round her neck, but lower down her flesh is exceeding white and delicate, so far as one could see.

As for her face, it is and appears to be very aged. It is long and thin, and her teeth are very yellow and unequal, compared with what they were formerly, so they say, and on the left side less than on the right. Many of them are missing so that one cannot understand her easily when she speaks quickly.

. . . She said that she was on the edge of the grave and ought to bethink herself of death, and suddenly she checked herself, saying, 'I think not to die so soon, Master Ambassador, and am not so old as they think'. I told her that God would preserve her yet for the good of her Realms and her subjects, and that she did wrong to call herself old so often as she did, and by God's grace her disposition was such that she had no occasion to call herself so. She answered me that Monsieur de Beaumont always said the same, that she did wrong to call herself by this word 'old', and verily, save for her face, which looks old, and her teeth, it is not possible to see a woman of her fine and vigorous disposition both in mind and body . . .

When anyone speaks of her beauty she says that she was never beautiful, although she had that reputation thirty years ago. Nevertheless she speaks of her beauty as often as she can.

62 A poem written by the Queen

When I was fair and young and favour graced me,
Of many was I sought their mistress for to be,
But I did scorn them all and answered them therefore,
Go, go, go, seek some other where,
    Importune* me no more.

How many weeping eyes I made to pine with woe,
How many sighing hearts I have no skill to show,
Yet I the prouder grew, and answered them therefore,
Go, go, go, seek some other where,
    Importune me no more.

Then spake fair Venus' son, that proud victorious boy,
And said, fine dame since that you have been so coy,
I will so pluck your plumes that you shall say no more,
Go, go, go, seek some other where,
    Importune me no more.

When he had spake these words such change grew in my breast,
That neither day nor night since that I could take any rest,
Then lo, I did repent of that I said before,
Go, go, go, seek some other where,
    Importune me no more.

63 The Queen's 'Golden Speech', November 30, 1601

About a hundred and fifty members of the House of Commons packed the Council room at Whitehall to hear Elizabeth's finest speech on her favourite themes of the relationship between the sovereign and her subjects, and the glories and responsibilities of rule.

I do assure you there is no prince that loves his subjects better, or whose love can countervail our love. There is no jewel, be it of never so rich a price, which I set before this jewel: I mean your love. For I do esteem it more than any treasure or riches; for that we know how to prize, but love and thanks I count unvaluable. And, though God hath raised me high, yet this I count the glory of my crown, that I have reigned with your

* to trouble or pester with requests (of love)

loves. This makes me that I do not so much rejoice that God hath made me to be a Queen, as to be a Queen over so thankful a people. Therefore, I have cause to wish nothing more than to content the subject; and that is a duty which I owe. Neither do I desire to live longer days than I may see your prosperity; and that is my only desire. And as I am that person that still yet under God hath delivered you, so I trust, by the almighty power of God, that I shall be His instrument to preserve you from every peril . . .

I know the title of a King is a glorious title; but assure yourself that the shining glory of princely authority hath not so dazzled the eyes of our understanding, but that we well know and remember that we also are to yield an account of our actions before the great Judge. To be a King and wear a crown is a thing more glorious to them that see it, than it is pleasant to them that bear it. For myself, I was never so much enticed with the glorious name of a King or royal authority of a Queen, as delighted that God hath made me His instrument to maintain His truth and glory, and to defend this Kingdom (as I said) from peril, dishonour, tyranny and oppression.

There will never Queen sit in my seat with more zeal to my country, care for my subjects, and that will sooner with willingness venture her life for your good and safety, than myself. For it is my desire to live nor reign no longer than my life and reign shall be for your good. And though you have had and may have many princes more mighty and wise sitting in this seat, yet you never had nor shall have any that will be more careful and loving . . .

This, Mr Speaker, I pray you deliver unto the House, to whom heartily recommend me. And so I commit you all to your best fortunes and further counsels. And I pray you, Mr Comptroller, Mr Secretary, and you of my Council, that before these gentlemen go into their countries, you bring them all to kiss my hand.

64 The Queen's final illness

A young relative of the Queen, Sir Robert Carey, described the beginning of her last illness.

When I came to court, I found the Queen ill disposed, and she kept her inner lodging; yet she, hearing of my arrival, sent for me. I found her in one of her withdrawing chambers, sitting low upon her cushions. She called me to her; I kissed her hand, and told her it was my chiefest happiness to see her in safety and in health, which I wished might long continue. She took me by the hand, and wrung it hard, and said, 'No, Robin, I am not well!' and then discoursed with me of her indisposition, and that her heart had been sad and heavy for ten or twelve days; and, in her discourse, she fetched not so few as forty or fifty great sighs. I was grieved at the first to see her in this plight: for, in all my lifetime before, I never knew her fetch a sigh, but when the Queen of Scots was beheaded . . . I used the best words I could to persuade her from this melancholy humour; but I found by her it was too deep rooted in her heart, and hardly to be removed.

From that day forwards she grew worse and worse. She remained upon her cushions four days and nights at the least. All about her could not persuade her, either to take any sustenance or go to bed . . . My Lord Admiral was sent for . . . [and] what by fair means, what by force, he got her to bed. There was no hope of her recovery, because she refused all remedies.

65 The Queen's coronation ring is removed

William Camden recorded the poignant moment during the last weeks of the Queen's life when her coronation ring had to be sawn off to relieve the pain in her finger.

Upon the last day of January [1603] which was a very windy and rainy day, she removed from Westminster to Richmond, there to enjoy and refresh herself in her old age, and more freely to attend the serving of God. Upon which day (whether thinking on her death, or presaging what would ensue), she happened to say to the Lord Admiral, whom she always dearly affected, 'My throne hath been the throne of kings, neither ought any other than he that is my next heir to succeed me'. And the courtiers observed, that she never before more frequented prayers and the service of God than now. Who also report that she then commanded that ring wherewith she had been as it were joined in marriage to her Kingdom at her Inauguration, and had never since taken off, to be filed off from her finger, because it was so grown into the flesh that it could not be drawn off. Which was taken as a sad omen, as if it portended that her marriage with the Kingdom, contracted by that ring, would now be dissolved.

James VI
of Scotland
who succeeded
Elizabeth
and became
James I
of England

66 The Queen and the mirror

This following account, written after the Queen's death, is of
doubtful authenticity, but it does nevertheless point to the
pathos of Elizabeth's crumbling image as a monarch endowed
with heavenly virtues and ageless beauty.

Now falling into extremity, she sat two days and three nights upon her
stool, ready dressed, and could never be brought by any of her Council to
go to bed, or to eat or drink . . . Afterward, in the melancholy of her
sickness, she desired to see a true looking-glass . . . which glass being
brought her, she fell presently into exclaiming against those which had so
much commended her, and took it so offensively, that some which before
had flattered her, durst not come into her sight.

67 The Hollow Crown

From *King Richard II* by William Shakespeare

Shakespeare was fascinated by the world of appearances and
deceptions in which a monarch moved, and by the
relationship between the king's public role-playing and his
private self.

from Act 4, scene 1

Give me that glass, and therein will I read.
No deeper wrinkles yet? Hath sorrow struck
So many blows upon this face of mine
And made no deeper wounds? O, flatt'ring glass,
Like to my followers in prosperity,
Thou dost beguile me! Was this face the face
That every day under his household roof
Did keep ten thousand men? Was this the face,
That, like the sun, did make beholders wink?. . .
A brittle glory shineth in this face.
As brittle as the glory is the face,
For there it is, cracked in an hundred shivers.

from Act 3, scene 2

                                    . . . within the hollow crown
That rounds the mortal temples of a king,
Keeps Death his court, and there the antic sits,
Scoffing his state and grinning at his pomp,
Allowing him a breath, a little scene,
To monarchize, be feared, and kill with looks,
Infusing him with self and vain conceit,
As if this flesh which walls about our life,
Were brass impregnable: and humoured thus,
Comes at the last, and with a little pin
Bores through his castle wall, and farewell king!
Cover your heads, and mock not flesh and blood
With solemn reverence, throw away respect,
Tradition, form, and ceremonious duty,
For you have but mistook me all this while:
I live with bread, like you, feel want,
Taste grief, need friends – subjected thus,
How can you say to me, I am a king?

68 The Queen's death

From William Camden's history of the Queen's reign

. . . she would sit silent, refrain from meat, fixing her mind wholly upon her meditations, and would not endure any talk unless it were with the Archbishop of Canterbury, with whom she often prayed with great fervency and devotion until by little and little her speech failed her . . . Then being put in mind by the Archbishop to think upon God; 'That I do,' said she, 'neither doth my mind at all wander from him.' And when she could no longer pray with her tongue, with hands and eyes lift up she directed the thoughts of her pious heart to God . . .

On the 24th of March, being the Eve of the Annunciation of the Blessed Virgin, she (who was born on the Eve of the Nativity of the Blessed Virgin) was called out of the prison of her earthly body to enjoy an everlasting country in Heaven, peaceably and quietly leaving this life, having reigned 44 years, 4 months, and in the 70th year of her age; to which no King of England ever attained before.

69 Public reaction to the Queen's death

Thomas Dekker, a writer of plays and tracts, described the effect of Elizabeth's death on the nation.

The report of her death, like a thunderclap, was able to kill thousands. It took away hearts from millions. For having brought up, even under her wing, a nation that was almost begotten and born under her, that never shouted any other *Ave* than for her name, never saw the face of any prince but herself, never understood what that strange outlandish word 'change' signified – how was it possible but that her sickness should throw abroad an universal fear, and her death an astonishment?. . .

Never did the English nation behold so much black worn as there was at her funeral . . . Her hearse, as it was borne, seemed to be an island swimming in water, for round about it there rained showers of tears; about her deathbed, none, for her departure was so sudden and so strange that men knew not how to weep because they had never been taught to shed tears of that making. They that durst not speak their sorrows whispered them; they that durst not whisper, sent them forth in sighs. Oh, what an earthquake is the alteration of a state!

70 Epilogue

From John Stow's *Annals*

The state of this Great Queen throughout the whole course of her most flourishing reign, was (as in part you have seen shadowed already) so beautified and strengthened with all honourable perfections, both of Peace and War, as never any Monarch reigned with greater observance of her own, nor ruled with a more observed magnanimity toward foreign nations: insomuch, as if her incomparable virtues and praises were truly and exactly described, we are verily persuaded that future ages will somewhat doubt whether such celebration of her were not rather affectionately poetical, than faithfully historical.

A mourner at Queen Elizabeth's tomb

Vos autem sicut ho:
mines moriemini.
Psa: 82. 6. 7.

Oterq̄ quater q̄
beati.

FVI
ELIZA
BETHA

O quam te memorem virgo!

Sources

Numbered as the extracts are arranged in the book. Unless otherwise stated all titles were published in London.

1 Raphael Holinshed *The Chronicles of England, Scotland and Ireland* 1587, p.1172.
2 *Ibid*, p.1179.
3 Sir John Hayward *Annals of . . . Queen Elizabeth*, edited by John Bruce 1840, pp.6–7.
4 Roger Ascham *English Works*, edited by William Wright, Cambridge, 1970, p.219.
5 Quoted in Conyers Read *Mr Secretary Cecil and Queen Elizabeth* 1955, p.124.
6 Quoted in Harry T. Moore, (ed.) *Elizabethan Age* New York, 1965, p.26.
7 Quoted in G.R. Elton *The Tudor Constitution* Cambridge, 1960, pp.15–16.
8 William Shakespeare *Troilus and Cressida*, Act 1, scene 3, lines 81 *ff* edited by Alice Walker, Cambridge, 1957.
9 T. Wright (ed.) *Queen Elizabeth and her Times* 1838, p.457.
10 *The Letters of Queen Elizabeth*, edited by G.B. Harrison 1935, p.174.
11 *Calendar of State Papers Spanish, 1568–79*. Quoted in J. Hurstfield and A. Smith (eds.) *Elizabethan People, State and Society* 1972, pp.143–4.
12 As note 7 above, pp.263–4.
13 *Ibid*, pp.266–7.
14 Quoted in William Rye *England as Seen by Foreigners* 1865, pp. 104–5.
15 Quoted in Roy Strong and Julia Oman *Elizabeth R* 1971, *p.25.*
16 Quoted in John Nichols *The Progresses and Public Processions of Queen Elizabeth* 1823 Volume 3, p.500.
17 Edmund Spenser *The Faerie Queene* Book V, Canto IX. See *Poetical Works*, edited by J.C. Smith and E. de Selincourt 1912, p.318.
18 William Camden *The History of . . . Elizabeth* 1675 edition, pp.26–7.
19 William Camden *Annals, or the Historie of . . . Elizabeth* 1635, pp.31–2.
20 *Memoirs of Sir James Melville*, edited by A. Francis Steuart 1929, pp.91–2 and 94.
21 As note 18 above, pp.268–9.
22 As note 10 above, p.174.
23 *The Poems of Queen Elizabeth I*, edited by Leicester Bradner, Providence, Rhode Island, 1964, p.5.
24 As note 16 above, Volume I, pp.105–6.
25 As note 7 above, pp.416–8.
26 As note 10 above, pp.203–4.
27 S. D'Ewes *Journals 1682* pp.328–9, quoted in J. Hurstfield and A.

Smith *op. cit.* note 11 above, p.115.
28 *De Maisse, A Journal* . . . translated and edited by G.B. Harrison and R.A. Jones 1931, pp.21–2.
29 As note 20 above, pp.95–7.
30 Quoted in Roy Strong *Mary, Queen of Scots* 1972, p.74.
31 As note 10 above, p.181.
32 Quoted in J.E. Neale *Elizabeth I and her Parliaments, 1584–1601* 1957, pp.117, 119 and 127.
33 Quoted in H. Ellis (ed.) *Original Letters* second series 1825, Volume III, p.113. See also M.M. Maxwell-Scott *The Tragedy of Fotheringhay* Edinburgh, 1905, Appendices.
34 As note 10 above, p.188.
35 John Stow *The Annales, or Generall Chronicle of England* 1615, p.746 *ff.*
36 Quoted in Patrick Tytler *Life of Sir Walter Raleigh* 1840, pp.89–90.
37 As note 35 above, p.750 *ff.*
38 Quoted in Paul Johnson *Elizabeth I* 1974, p.320.
39 John Speed *The Historie of Great Britaine* . . . 1611, p.1214.
40 As note 38 above, p.207.
41 E.P. and Conyers Read, (eds.) *John Clapham: Elizabeth of England* Philadelphia, 1951, p.89.
42 *Thomas Platter's Travels in England 1599*, translated and introduced by Clare Williams, 1937, pp.194–5.
43 As note 20 above, p.96.
44 As note 28 above, p.95.
45 Quoted in J.E. Neale *Queen Elizabeth* 1934, p.207.
46 As note 16 above, Volume III, p.80.
47 *The Black Book of Warwick*, transcribed and edited by T. Kemp, Warwick, 1898, pp.95–7.
48 Sir John Harington *Nugae Antiquae*, selected by Henry Harington, 1804, Volume I, pp.314–16.
49 As note 35 above, p.697.
50 Quoted in E.K. Chambers *The Elizabethan Stage* 1923, Volume 1, p.161.
51 As note 16 above, Volume III, pp.136–7.
52 William Shakespeare. *King Henry VI, Part 3*, Act 2, scene 5, lines 21–54, edited by A.S. Cairncross 1964.
53 As note 45 above, p.324.
54 As note 35 above, pp.787–8.
55 Sidney Papers quoted in Paul Johnson *op. cit.* note 38 above, pp.400–1.
56 *Calendar of State Papers, Domestic Series, 1598–1601* 1869, pp.435–6.
57 As note 18 above, pp.604–5.
58 As note 35 above, p.791 *ff.*
59 *Ibid*, p.792; and as note 18 above, p.622.

60   As note 48 above, Volume I, pp.317–19.
61   As note 28 above, pp.25–6, 82, 38.
62   As note 23 above, p.7.
63   As note 32 above, pp.389–91.
64   *The Memoirs of Robert Carey*, edited by F.H. Mares, Oxford, 1972, pp.57–9.
65   As note 18 above, p.659.
66   As note 16 above, Volume III, p.612.
67   William Shakespeare *King Richard II*, Act 4, scene 1, lines 276 *ff.*, and Act 3, scene 2, lines 160–77, edited by John Dover Wilson, Cambridge, 1939.
68   As note 18 above, pp.660–1.
69   *Thomas Dekker, Selected Writings*, edited by E.D. Pendry, 1967, pp.33–4.
70   As note 35 above, p.1214.

Further reading

A selection of titles not included in the sources list. Unless otherwise stated all titles were published in London.

BECKINGSALE, B.W. (1967) *Burghley, Tudor Statesman.*
BECKINGSALE, B.W. (1963) *Elizabeth I.*
BYRNE, M. St Clare (1961) *Elizabethan Life in Town and Country* (Revised edition).
ELTON, G.R. (1974) *England under the Tudors* (Second edition).
FALLS, C. (1950) *Elizabeth's Irish Wars.*
HARRISON, G.B. (1937) *The Life and Death of Robert Devereux, Earl of Essex.*
HURSTFIELD, J. (1960) *Elizabeth I and the Unity of England.*
JENKINS, E. (1958) *Elizabeth the Great.*
JENKINS, E. (1961) *Elizabeth and Leicester.*
MORRIS, C. (1953) *Political Thought in England from Tyndale to Hooker* Oxford.
PLOWDEN, A. (1977) *Marriage with my Kingdom. The Courtships of Queen Elizabeth I.*
PLOWDEN, A. (1971) *The Young Elizabeth.*
ROWSE, A.L. (1950) *The England of Elizabeth.*

ROWSE, A.L. (1971) *The Elizabethan Renaissance: The Life of the Society*.
Shakespeare's England. An account of the Life and Manners of his Age,
Oxford, 1916 (2 vols.)
SMITH, Lacey Baldwin (1976) *Elizabeth Tudor Portrait of a Queen*.
WILLIAMS, N. (1972) *All the Queen's Men. Elizabeth I and her Courtiers*.
WILLIAMS, N. (1967) *Elizabeth I, Queen of England*.
WILLIAMSON, J.A. (1959) *The Tudor Age*. (Second edition).
WILSON, C.H. (1970) *Queen Elizabeth and the Revolt of the Netherlands*.

Illustration acknowledgements

National Portrait Gallery: page 2, 22, 23, 33, 34, 42, 59, 64, 95, 101
Arthur Lockwood: page 11, 14/15, 53, 54, 56, 85, 91
Royal Commission on Historical Monuments
National Monuments Record: page 12
British Museum: page 17, 67, 69
Staatliche Kunstsammlungen Kassel: page 29
Ashmolean Museum, Oxford: page 32
Mansell Collection: page 37, 47, 50, 74/75, 76, 79, 87, 92, 103, 117
Lord Salisbury: page 45
Shakespeare's Birthplace Trust Library: page 106

Using the book for dramatic presentation

A selection of the writings collected in this book was presented in the Royal Shakespeare Theatre as an anthology recital for two male readers (an older voice contrasting with that of a younger man), one female reader and a lutanist/singer who played Elizabethan music. I hope some school, college or theatre groups will use the material for similar dramatic purposes, adapting it, if desired, for more than three readers.

For a stage presentation, a selection should be made from the writings to form two halves of about fifty and forty-five minutes respectively, with an interval in between. The basic shape of the anthology should be followed as it now stands, although over a third of the present material will have to be omitted. The more didactic extracts should be removed, the focus should be kept firmly on the Queen, and the aim must be to present an entertainment rather than a history lesson.

In making a selection for dramatic presentation I suggest that the following extracts are omitted: Numbers 5, 7, 8, 12–13, 24–8, 34, 39, 42, 46–7 and 64. The remainder will form the programme but several of the longer pieces may need some cutting, such as Numbers 32–3, 56, 58 and 61.

Music will make an important contribution to the overall balance of the programme, giving period atmosphere, heightening emotion at certain points and relaxing the audience (Elizabethan prose and poetry, not least the Queen's own involved manner of writing, place special demands on a modern audience). Six varied Elizabethan songs or instrumental pieces should be chosen for each half, related in theme and mood to their contexts. (If the reading is being prepared as a classroom exercise, students may enjoy putting a selection of songs and pieces onto tape, taken from the many recordings of Elizabethan music that are available on the market. Fanfares and other musical effects could also be included on a tape.)

The staging should be kept simple with a throne-like chair placed centre and down-stage for the woman reader who plays Elizabeth, and chairs placed in a slight horse-shoe position on either side for the other readers and the musician. Stage moves should not be too fussy and will be worked out by the director and the readers. Some pieces are clearly best read seated, some from a standing position, and others invite more than one move during presentation. Certain extracts will be more effective if they are presented by more than one reader, including Numbers 1, 2, 3, 15, 16, 35, 37, 58 and 59. The recital may benefit, in many cases, if most of the short introductory headings of the individual pieces are retained as spoken narrative. Readers should be as familiar as possible with the material but they should perform from hand-held texts so that the convention of a dramatic reading is kept throughout.

Index of Persons